THE GAME COOK

THE GAME COOK

Carolyn Little

The Crowood Press

First published in 1988 by
The Crowood Press Ltd
Ramsbury, Marlborough
Wiltshire SN8 2HR

Paperback edition 1998

British Library Cataloguing-in-Publication Data

A catalogue record for this book is available from the British Library.

ISBN 1 86126 1586

Line illustrations by Pat Warren

Typeset by Qualitext Typesetting, Abingdon
Printed in Great Britain by Redwood Books, Trowbridge, Wiltshire

Dedication

For Crawford and my sons Jamie, David and Justin

CONTENTS

ACKNOWLEDGEMENTS

My special thanks to the following friends and relatives who contributed their recipes and gave invaluable help and support in numerous ways:

Sheila Anderson
Kathy Berman
Jake Blackwood
Isabel Campbell
Kate Duffin
Henry Gough-Cooper
Catherine Little
Sarah Lukas
Margie Luxmoore
Liz McGregor
Margaret McTurk
Pamela Mitchell
Pamela Pumphrey
Karen Sommer
Christina Stewart
Alison Turnbull
Robert and Mary Waugh
and, of course, Crawford

I would also like to thank Brother microwaves, and *Countrysport* and *Period Homes* magazines for their kind permission to reproduce recipes which they have featured previously.

PREFACE

The days when game cookery was limited to the realms of the private country house party or the farmer's house and keeper's cottage are long gone. Today everyone can eat game and in fact it is becoming increasingly popular. I believe the reasons for this include the decline of the great estates (which would not have considered the possibility of selling the game shot for profit), the birth of the syndicate shoots, the redistribution of wealth, the development of game farming for the table, a realistic approach to marketing to a mass market, and a host of other factors. Surely, however, at the end of the day what matters is that so many people have discovered that game is not only delicious and healthy eating but also, in relative terms, no more expensive than other meats.

The arrival of oven-ready game, prepacked and clearly labelled, is something that I regard as a mixed blessing. It makes no allowance for individual taste with regard to hanging times, and we have to rely on the knowledge of the game dealer in ageing the bird. On the other hand, it allows frozen game to be sold out of season, and it is so very convenient.

Whenever I look at those neatly packaged, oven-ready bundles, I cannot help thinking about my own introduction to game cookery on the grand scale. I had just married Crawford, who had recently finished his training in estate management. We were living in Langholm, where he worked for the Buccleuch Estates. One morning I had a visit from Liz Finlay, the factor's wife. Each year a party of Americans came over for the grouse shooting but at the last minute the agency cooks had let her down so she had come to ask me if I would help out. With another girl, Jane, we were to cater for 18 Americans and their various guests for a week. This sounded like money for old rope; however, I soon changed my mind on that score.

As Jane was to live in she was on breakfast shift and we both shared the lunch, afternoon tea and dinner production. Lunch involved boxloads of food being transported to the moor several miles away, followed by a frenzy of activity to be back in time to serve the ladies afternoon tea and prepare dinner.

On the warm morning of 12 August a Land Rover appeared with the first batch of grouse to be plucked and made ready for that evening's dinner. After the first dozen Jane and I were both feeling a bit off colour, and the prospect of another dozen made it worse. The sound of my beaten-up old Fiat coming up the drive was music to our ears. Crawford and a friend, Rhoderick Noble, emerged from the car and, rescuing us from our plight, completed the task at record speed. For quite some time after that I could raise little enthusiasm for grouse.

The week went well, but by the end of it I felt as if I had been on an intensive training course. The Americans had no complaints but one lady did puzzle us. Clad in expensive handmade Italian shoes and sporting a mink-lined raincoat on the moor, she would eat nothing but salted peanuts washed down with Pepsi at each meal. Whether this was out of loyalty to the then President Carter or not we never did discover!

What I did discover, in the months that followed, was that there was a lot more to game cookery than grousing about grouse. First there was the discovery of an entire roe buck hanging in the garage where our car should have been. Crawford had forgotten to mention it and conveniently made himself scarce as I sharpened my knives and learnt through trial and error how to deal with the carcass. With the autumn came a steady flow of pheasants and other game; with spring came salmon, trout and sea trout, but this is another story.

My early trials and tribulations as a game cook were due, very largely, to a lack of guidance and good recipes (other than established family favourites). Family favourites can quickly lose their appeal and I was soon looking for greater variety. Disasters and tragedies were far from being unknown. I hope this book will help you to avoid such disappointments. I have tried to write it to cover a wide range of needs and interests, from the novice faced with the first brace of unhung, unplucked and uncleaned pheasants, to those who have eaten game all their lives and are seeking new ideas; I hope it will encourage you towards a more adventurous approach to game cookery.

INTRODUCTION

Game is becoming ever more widely available. In addition to the traditional game dealer or farmer, many high-street shops are now stocking game and some supermarkets are also taking up the challenge, offering a variety of oven-ready game.

The advantages of going to a game dealer are significant ones. Game dealers are specialists in their field and should be able to advise you not only on choosing and cooking game but also as to when it was shot. This will affect hanging times if, say, the bird you buy on Friday was shot on Wednesday and therefore has already been hung for two days. For an additional fee most game dealers will provide a plucking and drawing service for the birds they are selling and, for a slightly larger fee, will undertake the task of making your own game oven-ready.

The game bought in supermarkets is usually clearly labelled with its age, species and a suggested mode of cookery. This, and the fact that supermarkets will only accept game that is in prime condition, makes it a more expensive proposition than game bought from the game dealer.

Shooting folk also may have recourse to the game dealer or supermarket. There are many who do not care for a house full of flying feathers and down. Even the rough-shooter, who bags an assortment of species, may need to top up his supply and add quantity to variety. On the other hand there is little in the way of variety in the home of the syndicate shooter who returns bearing, with monotonous regularity, a brace of pheasants and nothing else.

COOKING GAME

Game is no more difficult to cook than any other meat or poultry. Once the game has been hung and is ready for the pot, wipe the birds and joints inside and out with a damp cloth. If there is a danger that the game may have been overhung or is strong smelling, dip it in a solution of water and vinegar or place half an onion inside the body cavity during cooking to absorb the smell.

There are no hard and fast rules about cooking game. The recipes for the species are nearly all interchangeable. The exception to this is the rabbit which needs strongly flavoured additions to the pot to bring out a good flavour. Other game has a strong, distinctive flavour and lends itself well to the addition of fruits and wines.

Marinades are invaluable in the case of an older game bird and nearly always essential when preparing hare and venison to make the joints more tender and moist.

As game has little or no fat, the addition of bacon or stock to some recipes prevents it from drying out during cooking. Where possible, birds should be cooked upside down so that the moisture flows down into the drier breasts.

A pheasant may have a covering of yellow fat. This must be removed before cooking or it will give the bird a bitter, metallic taste.

Pots and casseroles with tight-fitting lids are a boon to the game cook. Roasting bags, foil, greaseproof and waxed paper all help to contain the juices in the meat and keep it moist. A pair of jointing shears is an invaluable piece of equipment which makes the task of jointing birds infinitely easier. While young game can be successfully roasted or grilled with thorough basting, the older game benefits from longer cooking at lower temperatures.

All game that has been badly damaged should be dealt with as soon as possible. The hanging times should be reduced and traces of shot and bruising cut out and removed. It is best to keep these joints for casseroling, terrines or soup. A roast pheasant with half a leg and teeth marks from a hard-mouthed dog does not look very appealing on the table!

AGEING

Before you can decide how long to hang game or upon the method of cooking it, you will need a rough idea of its age. There is only one reliable method of judging the age of all game birds: the bursa test.

Bursa Test

All young game birds, on the upper side of the vent, have a small, blind-ended passage called a bursa. In all species the bursa will reduce or close completely with sexual maturity. To test for this, open out the vent area with the thumb and carefully insert a blunt-ended matchstick into the passage. In a large game bird, such as a young pheasant, the matchstick will penetrate the bursa up to a depth of 2cm/¾in and slightly less far for the smaller species.

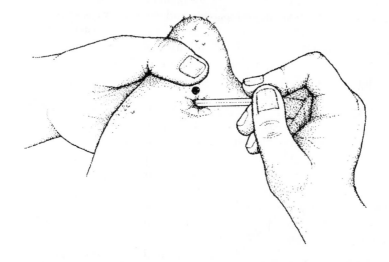

Although this test is perfectly all right to carry out if you have been presented with game birds at home, I am not sure whether your local game dealer would appreciate this performance in his busy shop! It might be politic to ask his opinion, especially if you have gone with the idea of purchasing a brace of young birds for roasting. An older bird simply will not roast or grill in the usual way without being tough.

Other pointers to look for when ageing birds are the feathers and, in the case of the pheasant, the spurs and feet. As a general rule the outer primaries on flight feathers of all game birds (except pheasant) are more pointed in a young bird and, in an older one, more blunted or rounded.

The young cock pheasant has soft, rounded spurs which become sharp and pointed in his second year. The young hen pheasant has soft feet which become rough and hardened with age.

Ageing game is perhaps the most difficult aspect of all, so err on the side of caution; if in doubt, casserole it!

HANGING

All the hanging times on the chart are approximate, as much depends on temperature of storage, personal preference as to 'gamey' flavour and the

Game Chart

Game	Shooting Seasons	Approximate hanging times
Pheasant	1 Oct–1 Feb	3–10 days
Grouse	12 Aug–10 Dec	2–7 days
Woodpigeon	All year	No hanging required
Partridge	1 Sept–1 Feb	2–8 days
Woodcock	England & Wales 1 Oct–31 Jan Scotland 1 Sept–31 Jan	3–12 days
Snipe	12 Aug–31 Jan	3–12 days
Rabbit	All year	No hanging required
Hare	All year, but may not be offered for sale March-July	7–14 days
Teal	1 Sept–20 Feb below high tide mark	1–2 days
Mallard	1 Sept–31 Jan elsewhere	1–2 days
Widgeon		1–2 days

Number of servings	Freezing Times (months)				
	whole	jointed	stocks & soups	pies & terrines	casseroles & stews
hen: 2 cock: 2–4	8	6	3	1–2	2–3
1–2	8	6	3	1–2	2–3
1	4	3	2	1–2	2–3
1	8	6	3	1–2	2–3
1	4	4	2	1–2	2–3
1–2 birds per person	4	4	2	1–2	2–3
2–3	6	6	3	1–2	2–3
6–8	8	6	4	2–3	2–3
1–2 birds per person	6	4	3	1–2	2–3
2–3	8	6	3	1–2	2–3
1–2	8	6	3	1–2	2–3

age of the game. The older the game, the longer it needs to be hung for tenderising and producing a gamey flavour, whereas young birds will lose their delicate flavour if overhung. Many would argue that pheasant should be hung for at least a month, but unless the circumstances are extreme I would advise against this; as with other meat, game can go off, becoming toxic or at the very least difficult to digest. If you are buying game from the game dealer, check how long it has been hung first.

In Britain it is traditional to hang game birds by their necks. On the Continent, however, game is hung by the feet or by one leg. Whichever method you adopt is purely a matter of preference. Some Americans prefer not to hang certain game at all, and although this may be all right with a young bird early in the season, I should imagine that later on game would be as tough as old boots if treated in this way.

Hares are the exception to the rule. They must be hung by their back legs with a cup or a bowl placed underneath the head to catch the blood. A teaspoonful of vinegar in the bowl will prevent the blood from congealing.

The one essential to remember is that all game should be hung individually to ensure that air is able to circulate freely. Birds that are wet, damaged or that have been bundled together will start to sweat and go off more quickly, and so special care should be taken to keep these in an airy atmosphere.

The ideal hanging place is a cool and darkened shed, or even the garage, preferably without the addition of exhaust fumes! Hang high, well out of the way of dogs, cats, mice and small boys with dart guns, catapults and the like!

All this may seem like a very confusing issue but there is a basic guideline to remember, and that is that young game needs less hanging than old, and that the bigger the game, the longer it needs.

PLUCKING

This should be done outside in some sheltered area out of the wind. With apron and wellies on, sit yourself on a stool. Some people like to pluck the feathers into a bin or box but I find the best method, if a little undignified, is to put my feet into a dustbin liner and pull it up to knee height. This helps to control the amount of flying feathers and down.

Place the bird across one knee with the head towards the bag. Start by

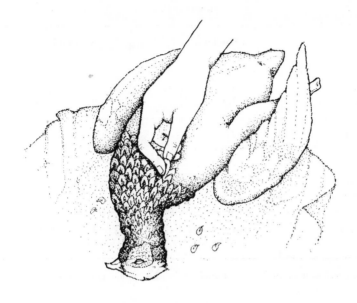

pulling out the wing feathers. If they are difficult to pull out, dip them in boiling water to soften the skin and this should ease the plucking. Pluck the body from tail to head against the feather growth if possible, but if the skin is in danger of tearing it is best to pluck from head to tail. Use pliers or tweezers to remove very stubborn feathers. The feathers of well-hung birds come out easily but the skin is especially delicate and much care is needed. Most of the remaining down will come away by rubbing gently with a damp cloth, but failing this hold the bird over a gas flame or candle to singe, taking care not to burn the skin. Cut off the feet. Reserve the tail feathers from a cock pheasant for decoration or, if you feel so inclined, keep them for a floral decoration with dried flowers; they have a good colour.

Most game dealers provide, for a small fee, a plucking, drawing and trussing service, if required.

Deer Chart

Shooting Seasons		
Type	**England**	**Scotland**
Red stags hinds	1 Aug–30 April 1 Nov–28 Feb	1 July–20 Oct 21 Oct–15 Feb
Fallow bucks does	1 Aug–30 April 1 Nov–28 Feb	1 Aug–30 April 21 Oct–15 Feb
Sika stags hinds	1 Aug–30 April 1 Nov–28 Feb	1 July–20 Oct 21 Oct–15 Feb
Roe bucks does	1 April–31 Oct 1 Nov–28 Feb	1 April–20 Oct 21 Oct–31 March

Different seasons apply in the Irish Republic. Further information can be obtained from The British Deer Society.

Goose Chart

Type	Shooting Seasons	Approximate hanging times
Pink footed goose	As for duck	10–21 days
Greylag goose	As for duck	10–21 days
Canada goose	As for duck	10–21 days
White fronted goose	England & Wales As for duck Scotland Fully protected	10–21 days

Different seasons apply in Northern Ireland, and in the Republic of Ireland. All giblets for freezing should be packed seperately and used within 2–3 months.

	Freezing Times (months)		
joints	stocks & soups	pies & terrines	casseroles & stews
8–10	3	1–2	4–6
8–10	3	1–2	4–6
8–10	3	1–2	4–6
8–10	3	1–2	4–6

Number of servings	Freezing Times (months)				
	whole	jointed	stocks & soups	pies & terrines	casseroles & stews
5–6	6	4	3	1–2	2–3
6–8	6	4	3	1–2	2–3
7–9	6	4	3	1–2	2–3
6	6	4	3	1–2	2–3

DRAWING

With a sharp knife or scissors cut off the bird's head at the top of the neck. Peel back the skin and cut the neck off close to the body and carefully draw out the windpipe and crop. As the crop may be full of food, care should be taken when removing it.

Make a small cut from the vent towards the abdomen, just big enough to get two fingers inside. Carefully remove the heart, gizzard, liver, gall bladder and intestines. Reserve the gizzard, heart, neck and liver (unless it is discoloured) for stock. Discard the intestines. Remove the vent. Check for and remove any shot. Wipe the bird inside and out with a damp cloth or kitchen towel.

To remove the tendons from the larger birds carefully cut the skin around the knee joint. Break the joint and pull out the tendons. If they will not come, carefully hook them out one by one with a skewer, and discard.

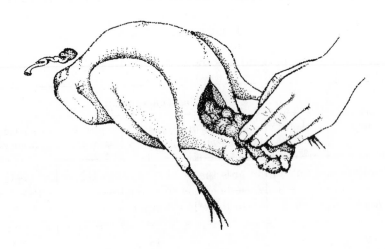

SKINNING

Birds

This is infinitely easier than plucking and I am silently relieved when presented with a bird that has been damaged or is only suited for a pie, casserole or terrine. To skin a whole bird, first cut off the head and wings. Cut the skin along the breastbone and carefully peel it back and round in one piece.

If the bird is small, such as the woodpigeon, and you are only going to use the breasts, simply cut along the breastbone with a sharp knife. Peel back the skin to expose the breasts and carefully cut out round the sides and ribs and remove them.

Rabbit

Rabbit must be paunched as soon as possible, preferably as soon as it has been shot. Before this can be done any urine in the bladder must be expelled by pressing your thumb in a downward motion towards the vent. With a sharp knife cut the rabbit's belly skin from the vent to the sternum. Holding the hind legs and ears, flick the rabbit's intestines out on to a newspaper. This is the least messy way to do it but, if the intestines are stubborn, remove them by hand. Keep the kidneys, liver and heart for stock if required.

Place the rabbit, belly up, on a newspaper. Cut off the feet and make a small cut around the tail. Carefully peel off the skin, starting with the hindquarters. Pull the skin back towards the head, peel back over the front legs and pull up towards the head. Cut off the head and tail and discard with the skin. Wash the rabbit in cold water and leave to soak in cold, salted water for two to three hours before cooking or freezing.

Hare

Hare is paunched after skinning which makes it a messier job, especially if you want to collect the blood for soups or gravy.

Firstly, cut off the feet. Place the hare, belly up, on a newspaper. Pinch up the belly skin and with a sharp knife make a small incision, taking great care not to puncture the body cavity. Peel back the skin around the hind legs. Make another cut around the tail and peel the skin

back towards the head. Remove the skin from the front legs and pull up towards the head. Cut off the head and tail and discard with the skin.

Cut the hare carefully up the middle towards the rib cage, taking care not to penetrate the diaphragm. Draw out the intestines and, keeping the liver and kidneys, discard the rest. Cut the diaphragm and keep any blood that has collected there and in the rib cage. Retain the heart for stock and discard the rest. Remove any remaining membrane.

Wash the hare in cold water and leave to soak for two to three hours in cold, salted water before cooking or freezing.

Add a tablespoon of vinegar to the blood and keep it in the fridge or freezer until further use.

TRUSSING

Trussing helps to prevent the bird from drying out during cooking. It also has cosmetic benefits in that the end result looks good on the table and the bird is easier to carve. Although it is a bit of a fiddle as, unlike a supermarket turkey, the game bird is anything but uniform in size, shape or condition, it is nevertheless worth the effort in doing the job well.

Stuff the bird if required. Place the bird breast down on the work surface. Fold the neck skin down over the back and pull back the wings close to the body, securing the skin if possible. Secure the wings by pushing a skewer into one wing, through the body and out through the other wing.

Turn the bird on its back. Make a small slit in the skin above the vent. Take a piece of string and wind it twice around the legs and parson's nose and tie securely.

For smaller birds use wooden cocktail sticks to secure the wings and legs.

FREEZING

All game freezes well, whether in its plucked or skinned and drawn state, or cooked in the form of a soup, casserole, terrine or pie. On occasion, when time has been short and the game in danger of being overhung, I have frozen birds intact. This, while convenient at the time, does mean that it will not store for so long and, once thawed, must be plucked, drawn and cooked as soon as possible.

As with other foods for the freezer the art is in wrapping the game securely and ensuring that the air is expelled from the bag, so avoiding the drying out of the food and possible freezer burn. Packages must be marked clearly with date, type and weight of the food. To save time it is a good idea to suggest a mode of cookery on the bag so that you don't end up with two young birds saved for a special occasion, when you wanted to make a casserole.

In rare moments of organisation, or perhaps in pre-children days when time was not so short, I kept a notebook on the side of the freezer marked 'FREEZER CONTENTS' containing all the relevant information regarding date, approximate servings etc. and I took pride in knowing exactly what I had in store. Those days are long gone although I promise to resurrect this efficient system every time I defrost the freezer (my eldest child was born in 1981) – maybe next time!

Game can be stored for longer uncooked than cooked, large joints for longer than small ones (see chart). The basic essential for freezing is good, sturdy packaging in the form of heavy-duty freezer bags, foil, greaseproof paper, tags or bag-sealer and labels clearly marked with a waterproof marker pen.

Whole birds should have their legs wrapped securely in foil or greaseproof paper to avoid sharp edges from piercing the bags. Alternatively, wrap the whole bird in foil and pack into a strong freezer bag. Jointed birds should be treated in the same way.

Game that has been badly damaged should be cooked in a casserole, terrine or soup as soon as possible and frozen in that form. Heavy-duty margarine boxes or freezer tubs are ideal for these. Leave 1–2cm/½–1in head space as the food will expand during freezing. Giblets have a shorter freezer life of about two months and can be stored in margarine tubs. Livers for terrines should be packed separately from the giblets.

Soups and casseroles will keep for up to three months in the freezer but a terrine is best used within six weeks. Highly spiced food does not store well and should not be kept for more than a month.

Any recipe that includes cream, eggs or milk is best frozen before they are added.

Game pies can be cooked before freezing but they are superior if they are made a day or two in advance and kept in the fridge.

Venison freezes well and most joints when packaged properly will keep for up to nine months.

THAWING

I am definitely of the old-fashioned brigade when it comes to this. Even with the invention of the microwave's defrost facility, I prefer to let uncooked joints thaw out slowly and naturally and am yet to be convinced that food tastes as good when it is quickly thawed. For cooked soups and casseroles the microwave is definitely the answer to a hot meal in minutes and I applaud this modern convenience in enabling us to get on with other things and still have time to enjoy a good meal.

MICROWAVING

As I have already said, we are now blessed with the invention of the microwave. For the purpose of this book I was kindly lent a Brother Hi-speed MF2100 for a trial period. To be honest, I didn't know how I could cope without it by the end of six months, but I used it purely for convenience in defrosting and reheating food quickly. Yes, it would roast a bird and make it look all golden brown in a fraction of the time and, yes, I could produce a casserole in thirty minutes, but the flavour and texture of the game left a lot to be desired.

Game on the whole needs care in cooking and often benefits from the long, slow methods which produce a full flavour and good texture.

The microwave was wonderful for producing a quick stock, soup or sauce, or for heating the baked beans, but there is ultimately no substitute in the first stage of meal preparation for a conventional oven.

CHAPTER 1

PHEASANT

(1 October–1 February)

Few could fail to recognise the cock pheasant. He looks distinctly oriental with his dark, metallic green head, bright red wattles around the eye and long, trailing tail. Body plumage varies from burnished gold to deep purple. A proud and impressive bird, he may measure nearly a yard from the point of his beak to the tip of his tail.

The hen looks decidedly drab by comparison. She is soberly coloured in shades of brown. The basic colour may be very light or very dark (in the melanistic mutant both the cock and hen are the colour of dark chocolate, flecked with black).

The pheasant was originally an Asian marshland bird, two of the main varieties being known as the Chinese and Mongolian pheasant, both having white on the neck. Although British pheasants may also live on fens and marshlands, the majority have taken to roosting in woodlands: a ground-roosting pheasant is an all too easy target for a fox.

Wild pheasants can be a great success on the light soils of some eastern counties, but in other areas shoots have to rely on rearing and release to top up the wild population. The pheasant has lent itself so well to this artificial method that it has become the mainstay of British shooting. Millions of pheasants are released on shoots throughout Britain each year. They thrive almost everywhere in Britain except on barren moorland.

The Game Conservancy tells us that 85 per cent of game birds shot, and therefore cooked and eaten, are pheasants. It is interesting to note that even though we rely so heavily upon the reared bird, wild birds still make up half the national bag.

Wild pheasants are great gleaners of the stubbles for spilt grain but they have very catholic tastes and will feed on a wide variety of foods. Grain, berries and beech mast are taken along with such items as wireworms, leatherjackets and even field mice and lizards, given the chance.

Reared birds are fed almost exclusively on grain. The keeper walks a tightrope between feeding too little, which will cause the birds to stray, or too much, which will make them fat. Besides the extra feed bill nobody wants a fat bird, neither the sportsman nor the cook who must remove all traces of yellow fat under the skin before cooking.

The only infallible way to age a pheasant is the bursa test (*see* Introduction). However, as a rough guide, a cock bird in its first season has short, rounded spurs. These become more pointed in the second year and long and sharp in subsequent years. A young hen has pliable feet that become roughened with age.

There are differing opinions on how long to hang a pheasant. Crawford's family still tell the tale of old Uncle Walter who, having nailed his pheasants to the barn wall through the loose skin on their necks, would not have them cooked until they had rotted and fallen! He was, I think, very lucky to survive such toxic material. The longest that we have ever hung pheasant was during a very cold spell in Langholm, when four brace were hung in an outside larder for five weeks – they were deep-frozen the whole time. Once they had been brought into the house and thawed out slightly, the insides came away in one whole frozen block. For more normal hanging times refer to Introduction! Pheasants are presented and sold by the brace, normally a cock and a hen. The hen is supposed to have a better flavour but I have not found this myself. Young pheasant will roast or grill well, older birds are best kept for casseroles and terrines. Where possible the birds should be cooked upside down, sitting on their breasts, to keep the meat moist.

Pheasant Soup

Serves 6   Cooking time: 1–1½ hours

1 pheasant
bouquet garni
75g/3oz butter
1 large onion, chopped
100g/4oz carrot, chopped
100g/4oz turnip, chopped
flour
15ml/1 tablespoon tomato purée
150ml/¼ pint wine
salt and pepper
150ml/¼ pint cream

Pre-heat oven to 180°C/350°F/Gas Mark 4

---

1   Place the whole bird in a large casserole dish, cover completely with water and add the bouquet garni. Cover the dish and place in the oven for 1–1½ hours.

---

2   When the pheasant is cooked, remove the bones and chop the flesh into small cubes. Retain the stock.

---

3   Melt the butter in a pan over a low heat and gently simmer the vegetables in it until tender. Add enough flour to absorb all the butter. Gradually pour the stock over the roux, stirring continuously. The amount of stock needed varies according to personal taste.

---

4   Stir in the tomato purée and wine. Add the chopped pheasant, heat through and season to taste. Stir in the cream immediately before serving.

Suggested accompaniment: Crusty French bread.

Pheasant Terrine

Serves 6   Resting time: 1 hour   Cooking time: 25 minutes, 1½–2 hours

This terrine is best stored for at least 3 days before use.

1 pheasant
700g/1½lb belly pork with rind
    removed and reserved
2 eggs, beaten
175ml/6fl oz port
1.5ml/¼ teaspoon cinnamon
1.5ml/¼ teaspoon ground cloves
5ml/1 teaspoon salt
pepper
4 juniper berries, crushed
bacon rashers to line terrine
100g/4oz streaky bacon
2 bay leaves

Pre-heat oven to 180°C/350°F/Gas Mark 4

---

1   Roast the pheasant for 25 minutes. Remove it from the oven and allow to cool. Reduce the oven temperature to 150°C/300°F/Gas Mark 2.

---

2   Cut away the flesh from the bird and chop into 2.5cm/1in pieces. Finely mince the pork and mix the pheasant pieces into it together with the spices, seasonings, eggs and port. Leave to stand for 1 hour.

---

3   Line the bottom and sides of the terrine with bacon and spoon half the mixture into the dish. Cover this with half the streaky bacon. Spoon in the remaining pheasant mixture and cover with the rest of the bacon. Place the bay leaves on the top and cover the terrine with pork rind.

---

4   Put the terrine into a roasting tin half-filled with water. This helps to prevent the mixture from drying out and forming a hard crust. Cook in the oven for 1½–2 hours.

---

5   Take the terrine from the oven and remove the rind. Allow the dish to cool and store for at least 3 days before use.

Suggested accompaniment: Serve with French bread or toast and salad.

Potted Pheasant

Serves 4   Preparation time: 15 minutes

225g/8oz cooked pheasant (flesh
  only)
150g/5oz clarified butter – melted
  and allowed to cool slightly
sprinkling of paprika
sprinkling of nutmeg
salt and pepper
lemon juice

1   After making sure that the pheasant flesh is completely dry, chop it finely.
     Beat approximately 50g/2oz of the clarified butter into the pheasant along
     with the salt, pepper, paprika, nutmeg and a few drops of lemon juice.

2   Pack the mixture into very clean china pots leaving room for a 5mm/¼in
     deep covering of clarified butter. Pour the butter over to seal well. Chill.

To serve: Potted meats and game can be served in a variety of ways; as a
starter with toast or as a snack salad lunch.

Roast Pheasant

Serves 6   Cooking time: 45 minutes

1 brace young pheasant
100g/4oz butter
2 lemon wedges
streaky bacon
salt
freshly ground black pepper

Pre-heat oven to 190°C/375°F/Gas Mark 5

1   Place half the butter inside the birds. Season well with salt and pepper.
    Place a lemon wedge inside each bird.

2   Truss the pheasants well and brush all over with the remaining butter. Cover
    the breasts and legs with the bacon.

3   Put the birds in the oven and roast them for 35 minutes. Baste frequently.

4   Remove the bacon from the pheasants and cut each strip into 2.5cm/1in
    lengths. Put the bacon on a separate baking sheet and return it with the
    birds to the oven for a further 10 minutes.

To serve: Place the roasted birds on an ashet and surround it with the
traditional accompaniments of game chips, bacon strips, roast chestnuts and
decorate with watercress and a few tail feathers.

Suggested accompaniment: Traditionally, in addition to the above, these
would include gravy, bread sauce or fried breadcrumbs, and Brussels sprouts.

Olive-Stuffed Pheasant

Serves 6 Cooking time: 1 hour

1 brace pheasant

For the stuffing:
100g/4oz chicken livers
100g/4oz belly pork
200g/7oz green olives
30ml/2 tablespoons brandy
salt
freshly ground black pepper
100g/4oz streaky bacon
275ml/½ pint red wine

For the topping:
25g/1oz butter
100g/4oz almond flakes

For the gravy:
10ml/2 level teaspoons cornflour
water

Pre-heat oven to 220°C/425°F/Gas Mark 7

---

1 To make the stuffing, mince the chicken livers and belly pork. Chop half the olives and add them with the brandy to the chopped pork and liver. Season with salt and pepper and stir well. Stuff the birds with this mixture.

---

2 Bard the pheasants with bacon and put them into a large, flame-proof casserole. Pour the wine over the birds. Cover the casserole and place in the oven.

---

3 After 30 minutes remove the lid from the casserole and continue to cook uncovered for a further 25 minutes.

---

4 To make the topping, melt a little butter in a pan over a low heat and gently brown the almond flakes. Add the remaining olives to the pan and heat through.

5   Drain the birds from the casserole and place on a warm dish. To make gravy, mix the cornflour to a smooth paste with water. Add to the casserole and stir until it has thickened. Season to taste with salt and pepper.

To serve: Carve the pheasants thinly and serve the slices with the stuffing and gravy, and the almond and olive topping.

Suggested accompaniment: Baked or creamed potatoes, braised celery and broccoli.

Pheasant with Cranberries and Orange

Serves 4   Cooking time: 1 hour

1 brace pheasant
50g/2oz butter
150ml/¹/₄ pint game stock
150ml/¹/₄ pint fresh orange juice
45ml/3 tablespoons sugar
100g/4oz fresh cranberries
1 orange, peeled and segmented
salt
freshly ground black pepper

Pre-heat oven to 180°C/350°F/Gas Mark 4

---

1   Halve the pheasants. Melt the butter in a large frying pan and gently brown the birds all over.

---

2   Remove the birds from the pan and place them in a large, flame-proof casserole.

---

3   Pour the game stock and the fresh orange juice into the pan with the sugar and simmer over a low heat until the sugar has dissolved.

---

4   Add the cranberries and the orange segments. Season to taste with salt and pepper and continue to simmer, stirring continuously for 5 minutes. Pour over the birds.

---

5   Cover the casserole with a close-fitting lid and cook in the oven for 1 hour.

Suggested accompaniment: Buttered green noodles and sautéd button mushrooms.

Stuffed Pheasant Breast

Serves 4   Cooking time: 1¼–1½ hours

Breasts of 2 pheasants, boned
100g/4oz lambs liver, finely
   chopped
1 small onion, finely chopped
225g/8oz thinly cut smoked
   streaky bacon
butter

Pre-heat oven to 150°C/300°F/Gas Mark 2

1   Lay the breasts out on a flat surface.

2   In a bowl mix the liver, onion and 50g/2oz of the finely chopped bacon. Spread this mixture on to 2 of the breasts without going to the edges. Place the other breasts on the top.

3   Wrap the remaining bacon tightly round the breasts to form parcels, reserving 4 rashers to place along the length of the breasts.

4   Place the pheasant parcels in a heavy-based casserole. Dot with a little butter and cover tightly. Place the dish in the oven and cook for 1¼–1½ hours. The bacon should be well browned.

To serve: Place the parcels on an ashet and carve them into thick slices.

Suggested accompaniments: Bread sauce, a thin gravy, jacket potatoes and boiled carrots. Also serve cold with Waldorf salad and pickles.

Pheasant Joints in Crumbs

Serves 4   Cooking time: 15–20 minutes

4 pheasant joints
a little flour
1 egg, beaten
golden breadcrumbs
sunflower oil for frying

1   Lightly coat the joints with a little flour. Dip them into the beaten egg and completely cover with golden breadcrumbs.

2   Heat the oil in a chip pan or deep fat fryer and cook the joints until they are well browned and crispy (15–20 minutes).

3   Drain the joints and remove any excess oil by dabbing them with a piece of kitchen towel.

To serve: Serve immediately.

Suggested accompaniment: Creamed potatoes and broccoli in cheese sauce.

Pot-Roasted Pheasant

Serves 4   Cooking time: 2½–3 hours

1 cock pheasant
2 carrots, sliced
2 shallots
100g/4oz mushrooms, sliced
5ml/1 teaspoon mixed herbs
425ml/¾ pint stock
150ml/¼ pint cider
salt
freshly ground black pepper

Pre-heat oven to 150°C/300°F/Gas Mark 2

1   Place the pheasant in a large casserole and add the vegetables and herbs.

2   Pour the stock and cider over the pheasant and season well with salt and pepper.

3   Cover the casserole and cook in the oven for 2½–3 hours, or until tender. A little more stock may be added if necessary.

To serve: Place the pheasant on a serving dish. Spoon the vegetables and stock over the top.

Suggested accompaniments: Baked or Anna potatoes and savoy cabbage.

Pheasant with Celery

Serves 4   Cooking time: approx. 1½ hours

1 old cock pheasant
50g/2oz butter
2 medium onions, chopped
head of celery
200ml/7fl oz stock
200ml/7fl oz cream
salt
freshly ground black pepper

1   Melt the butter in a large pan over a low heat and brown the bird all over. Add the chopped onions.

2   Cover the pan with a tight-fitting lid and simmer gently for 45 minutes. Remove from the heat.

3   Chop the celery into 2.5cm/1in lengths and boil in salted water for 8–10 minutes before draining.

4   Add the stock, celery and cream to the pheasant. Season well with salt and pepper. Cover the pan and return to simmer for a further 45 minutes or until tender.

To serve: Place the pheasant on a serving dish and spoon the stock and vegetables over the top. Serve immediately.

Suggested accompaniment: Boiled potatoes, baked apple rings and mashed carrots.

Grilled Pheasant with Tarragon and Garlic

Serves 4   Cooking time: 15–20 minutes

1 young cock pheasant, jointed
    into 4 pieces
50g/2oz butter, melted
2 garlic cloves, crushed
salt
pepper
4 small sprigs tarragon

1   Add the crushed garlic to the melted butter and season with salt and pepper. Simmer for 1 minute.

2   Push a sprig of tarragon under the skin of each joint and brush the joints all over with the garlic butter.

3   Put the joints under a hot grill, basting frequently. Turn once and cook until golden brown for approximately 15–20 minutes.

To serve: Serve immediately on hot plates. A little garlic butter may be spooned over the joints.

Suggested accompaniments: Game chips or straws and a good crisp salad with garlic dressing.

Pheasant with Lentils

(This recipe was given to me by Mary Waugh)

Serves 8   Cooking time: approx. 1½ hours

1 brace pheasant
225g/8oz red lentils
butter
225g/8oz smoked streaky bacon
*   cut into 2.5cm/1in lengths*
2 sticks celery, finely chopped

2 large carrots, diced
1 small leek, chopped
1 onion, finely chopped
2 garlic cloves, crushed
200ml/7fl oz game stock
salt and pepper

Pre-heat oven to 180°C/350°F/Gas Mark 4

1   Boil the lentils in salted water for 10 minutes. Drain.

2   Roast the pheasants in the oven for 30 minutes. Remove the birds from the pan and place them on a dish to one side. Reserve the meat juices. Reduce the oven temperature to 150°C/300°F/Gas Mark 2.

3   Melt a little butter in a large, heavy-based casserole and gently cook the bacon, celery, carrots, leek, onion and garlic for 10 minutes, stirring continually.

4   Add the lentils, game stock and meat juices to the casserole and season well with salt and pepper. Bring to the boil, then reduce the heat and, stirring continually, simmer for 2–3 minutes.

5   Put the birds into the casserole. Cover with a tight-fitting lid and place in the oven. Cook for a further 40–50 minutes. Check occasionally; if the dish appears to be too thick, add a little more stock or some wine.

To serve: Joint each bird into 4 pieces and place on a deep serving dish. Pour lentil mixture over and serve.

Suggested accompaniment: Boiled rice and a green salad in tarragon dressing.

Tipsy Pheasant

(This recipe was given to me by Mary Waugh)

Serves 6   Cooking time: 1½ hours

1 brace pheasant
bacon
butter
salt and freshly ground black
*   pepper*
275ml/½ pint claret
3 bread slices
watercress sprigs

Pre-heat oven to 180°C/350°F/Gas Mark 4

---

1   Bard the birds with bacon and place them on a rack in a roasting tin. Dot all over with butter and season with salt and black pepper. Roast in the oven for about 40 minutes, until tender.

---

2   Pour the claret into the bottom of the roasting tin. Continue to cook the pheasant for 30–40 minutes, basting frequently.

---

3   Remove the crusts from the bread and cut the slices in half, diagonally. Fry them in melted butter until crisp and golden brown. Put the toasts on a hot ashet and place the birds on top. Keep them warm.

---

4   To make the gravy, add the mixed herbs to the liquid in the roasting dish and allow to simmer for 3–4 minutes.

---

5   Mix a little cornflour to a smooth paste with some water and add this to the pan, stirring continuously until the gravy has thickened. More claret can be added if required.

To serve: Serve the birds on the toasts with the gravy. Garnish with watercress sprigs.

Suggested accompaniment: Bread sauce, game chips, buttered sprouts and carrots.

Savoury Pheasant in Wine and Orange

(This recipe was given to me by Liz McGregor)

Serves 4–6   Cooking time: 1 hour

1 brace pheasant (including
  livers)
12 small onions
30ml/2 tablespoons oil
30ml/2 tablespoons butter
100g/4oz small mushrooms
50g/2oz flour
150ml/¼ pint chicken stock
150ml/¼ pint orange juice
150ml/¼ pint very dry white wine
salt and pepper
1 orange

Pre-heat oven to 180°C/350°F/Gas Mark 4

---

1   Finely chop the livers and two of the onions, mix together and place half the
    mixture inside each bird.

---

2   Heat the oil and butter in a large frying pan. Add the pheasants and brown
    them all over. Remove from the pan with a slotted spoon and transfer to a
    large casserole. Lightly fry the mushrooms for a few minutes before draining
    from the pan. Add these to the casserole too.

---

3   Sprinkle the flour into the frying pan and cook gently for a minute or two.
    Remove the pan from the heat and gradually stir in the stock, orange juice
    and wine. Bring to the boil and stir until the sauce thickens. Season to taste
    and pour into the casserole.

---

4   Boil the remaining onions in salted water until tender. Add to the casserole.
    Cover and cook in the oven for 1 hour.

To serve: Garnish with orange segments and watercress.

Pheasant in Rich Tomato Sauce

Serves 4   Cooking time: 1½–2 hours

1 brace pheasant
flour, seasoned with salt and
*   pepper*
butter

For the sauce:
75g/3oz butter
1 onion, chopped
1 carrot, chopped
2 sticks celery, chopped
4oz mushrooms, sliced
425ml/¾ pint good stock
400g/14oz tin of tomatoes
30ml/2 tablespoons tomato purée

Pre-heat oven to 180°C/350°F/Gas Mark 4

1   Halve the birds. Coat them with the seasoned flour and cook in melted butter in a frying pan.

2   When the pheasant is browned all over, remove from the frying pan and place in a large casserole.

The sauce:

1   Melt the butter over a low heat and gently cook the onion, carrot, celery and mushrooms.

2   Gradually blend in enough flour to absorb all the butter. Add the stock and cook for 2–3 minutes before adding the tinned tomatoes and tomato purée. Season to taste. Allow the sauce to simmer for 30 minutes, stirring occasionally.

3   Pour the sauce over the birds and cook in the oven for 1–1½ hours.

Suggested accompaniment: Boiled rice, green salad and garlic bread.

Stewed Pheasant with Sauerkraut

(This recipe was given to me by Henry Gough Cooper)

Serves 6   Total cooking time: 2 hours 45 minutes

1 brace pheasant
100g/4oz butter
1 onion, finely chopped
700g/2lb sauerkraut, washed and
  drained
8 juniper berries, crushed
275ml/½ pint white wine
chicken stock
salt and pepper
225g/8oz smoked sausage, sliced
150ml/¼ pint gin
75g/3oz salt pork, chopped

The sauerkraut:
Cooking time: 2 hours

---

1   Melt 75g/3oz butter in a large pan. Add the onion and cook gently for 1–2 minutes.

---

2   Add the sauerkraut and the juniper berries. Stir and lift the sauerkraut continuously for 12–15 minutes.

---

3   Stir in half the white wine and a little stock; season with salt and pepper. Cover and cook over a low heat for 1½ hours, adding more stock as necessary to keep moist but not liquid.

---

4   Now add the smoked sausage to the pan and cook for a further 15 minutes. Pour in half the gin. Heat through and turn on to a serving dish.

The pheasants and sauce:
Cooking time: 45 minutes

---

1   Melt the remaining butter in a stew pan. Add the salt pork and the pheasants and lightly brown all over.

---

2   Pour the rest of the gin over the birds and boil for 10 seconds, then cover the pan and simmer gently for 40 minutes. Remove the birds to keep warm.

---

3   Pour the remaining white wine into the pan. Boil and allow to reduce and thicken. Pour over the sauerkraut.

To serve: Pour the sauce over the sauerkraut and place the birds on top.

Suggested accompaniment: A little potato if required, but the dish is quite filling on its own.

Faisan au Verger

Serves 4   Cooking time: 1½ hours

This recipe originates from Normandy. It is quite delicious and provides an excellent method of cooking the older birds.

1 brace pheasant
a little seasoned flour
a little butter
3 sticks celery, chopped
1 medium sized onion, chopped
4oz mushrooms, sliced
2 cooking apples, peeled and cut
    into cubes

275ml/½ pint cider
some stock made from the giblets
150ml/¼ pint double cream
salt
freshly ground black pepper

Pre-heat oven to 180°C/350°F/Gas Mark 4

---

1   Wipe the birds over with a clean cloth. Cut each into 2 joints and coat in seasoned flour.

---

2   Melt the butter in a heavy-based casserole on the stove top and cook the pheasant joints until they are lightly browned all over. Remove them and set to one side.

---

3   Gently fry the celery and onion until soft and then add the mushrooms and apple. Continue cooking the mixture for a few minutes, stirring all the time. Mix in a little flour and gradually add the cider and some of the stock.

---

4   Return the birds to the casserole; cover and cook in the oven for 1–1½ hours. If the casserole seems to be drying out during the cooking, some more stock should be added.

---

5   Remove the dish from the oven, pour over the cream, season to taste and gently heat through on the stove top for 2 or 3 minutes.

To serve: The pheasant should be served straight from the casserole.

Suggested accompaniment: Plain boiled or duchesse potatoes, tomatoes and courgettes.

Marinated Pheasant Casserole

Serves 4   Marinating time: 8–10 hours   Cooking time: 1½ hours

1 old cock pheasant, trussed
25g/1oz butter
1 medium onion, chopped
2 carrots, diced
2 celery sticks, chopped finely
5ml/1 teaspoon mixed herbs
salt
freshly ground black pepper

For the marinade
275ml/½ pint dry red wine
30ml/2 tablespoons olive oil
5ml/1 teaspoon grainy mustard
5ml/1 level teaspoon dried
   tarragon
1 bouquet garni sachet or muslin
1 garlic clove, skinned
2 bay leaves

The marinade

1 Put all the marinade ingredients into a large bowl and mix well.

2 Season the pheasant with salt and pepper and place in the marinade. Cover and leave to steep for 8–10 hours, turning frequently.

The casserole:
Pre-heat oven to 150°C/300°F/Gas Mark 2.

1 Strain the pheasant, reserving the marinade.

2 Melt the butter in a large, flame-proof casserole and brown the pheasant all over. Remove from the casserole and add the vegetables and mixed herbs. Simmer for 5 minutes.

3 Return the pheasant to the casserole. Add the marinade and bring it to the boil.

4 Cover the dish and cook in the oven for 1½ hours.

To serve: Place the bird in a large dish. Spoon over all the vegetables and juice and serve immediately.

Suggested accompaniment: Roast potatoes and leaf spinach.

Herby Pheasant Croquettes

Serves 6   Cooking time: 10–15 minutes

450g/1lb cooked pheasant, finely
    minced
100g/4oz cooked ham, finely
    minced
15ml/1 tablespoon dried parsley
salt
finely ground black pepper
2 eggs
a little flour
100g/4oz breadcrumbs
oil for deep frying

---

1   Mix together the pheasant, ham and parsley. Season with salt and pepper. Beat the eggs and pour half into the pheasant mixture to bind it.

---

2   Divide the mixture into 12 portions. Form each portion into a ball and roll it on a lightly floured board. Dip each ball into the remaining egg mixture and coat it with breadcrumbs.

---

3   Deep fry these croquettes for 10–15 minutes or until golden brown.

To serve: Drain the croquettes on some kitchen roll, top with fresh parsley and serve immediately.

Suggested accompaniment: Straw potatoes, sauerkraut or pickled red cabbage, and demi-glacé sauce (see Chapter 11).

CHAPTER 2

RED GROUSE

(12 August–10 December)

It is not simply that the red grouse is the first game bird to come into season, and it is something more than the challenge presented by these fast, acrobatic birds; possibly it has something to do with the gathering of old friends and the spectacular moorland scenery; whatever the reason, few sportsmen who have met the grouse in his rolling kingdom of purple heather would not place him at the top of their list of favourites.

The grouse is a medium-sized game bird. It has reddish brown plumage speckled with white and black and a distinctive red comb over the eye which is more prominent in the cock. Both sexes have feathered legs and feet which some people like to have made into kilt pins and the like. Moorlands are never the same without the gurgling, rasping, 'go-back' call of the grouse.

The grouse season is not only the first to open but also the first to close, and even then, shooting will normally have stopped well before the legal closing of 10 December. There are two reasons for this. Firstly, the grouse may pair and choose nesting sites as early as late November. Secondly, grouse usually join into packs of hundreds of birds by October, and this makes shooting impractical.

The principal food of the grouse is ling heather. They eat the young green shoots as well as the flowers and seed heads which is possibly why grouse meat always tends to be darker and stronger flavoured than that of other game birds. Besides the staple diet of heather, they are also keen on foods such as blayberry, cranberry and the seeds of sorrel which, depending on their local availability, will add further distinctive flavours to the meat. The flavour of grouse also varies from region to region.

The most reliable way to age grouse is by the bursa test (*see* Introduction). The second best is by examining the outer flight feathers on the wing. In young birds the two outermost feathers will be pointed and, in some cases, the third feather will be shorter than the rest. In older grouse all the flight feathers will be blunt and of the same length.

It is not essential to hang young grouse. An older bird will require hanging but limit the hanging time as it can be warm even into October.

Young grouse are best roasted or split down the back and grilled. They are also suited to the barbecue, especially if you have a rôtisserie. The older birds make a good casserole or you could try a pot roast.

Grouse and Lettuce Soup

Serves 4   Cooking time: 1–1½ hours

1 grouse
5ml/1 teaspoon mixed herbs
salt and pepper
50g/2oz butter
2 medium onions, chopped
2 carrots, diced
2 heads lettuce, shredded
5ml/1 teaspoon cornflour
    (optional)
parsley or chives for garnish
cream (optional)

1   Place the grouse in a large pan and cover with water. Add the mixed herbs and season with salt and pepper. Bring the pan to the boil. Cover, lower the heat and simmer for 1–1½ hours until the grouse is very tender.

2   Remove the bird from the pan and put to one side to cool slightly before removing the flesh. Strain the stock into a bowl to make sure that there are no fragments of bone in it.

3   Melt the butter over a low heat in the pan and add the onion and the carrots. Simmer gently for 5 minutes. Then add the shredded lettuce and, stirring continuously, cook for a further 3–4 minutes.

4   Chop the grouse and add this to the pan. Pour in 1 pint of the stock and simmer for 10 minutes.

5   Blend the soup in a liquidiser or food processor or by hand through a sieve. If it appears thin a teaspoon of cornflour can be added at this stage. Then pour the soup back into the pan and reheat slowly, stirring all the time.

To serve: Pour the soup into a tureen and swirl with cream. Garnish with fresh, chopped parsley or chives.

Grouse Terrine

Serves 6–8   Cooking time: 1 hour 15 minutes

450g/1lb cooked grouse, chopped
900g/2lb belly pork, minced
175g/6oz streaky bacon
75ml/3fl oz red wine
1 clove garlic, crushed
salt and pepper
15ml/1 tablespoon port
2 bay leaves
lard or clarified butter (optional)

Pre-heat oven to 150°C/300°F/Gas Mark 2

---

1   Mince the belly pork with 50g/2oz bacon into a large bowl. Stir in the wine and port. Add the garlic and grouse. Season with salt and pepper.

---

2   Line the bottom and sides of a terrine with bacon and fill with the mixture. Cover with the remaining bacon and place the bay leaves on the top.

---

3   Place the dish on a rack in a roasting tin half-filled with water and cook in the oven for 1 hour 15 minutes.

---

4   Remove the bay leaves. Allow the dish to cool and seal with a layer of melted lard or clarified butter.

To serve: Remove the fat and serve with toast, or bread sticks, lemon wedges and a good, crisp salad.

Roast Grouse

Serves 2   Cooking time: 40–50 minutes

1 brace grouse
butter
salt and pepper
275ml/½ pint stock from giblets
15ml/1 tablespoon flour

Pre-heat oven to 170°C/325°F/Gas Mark 3

1   Place a dessertspoonful of butter inside the body cavity. Butter the breast and legs well and sprinkle with salt and pepper.

2   Place the grouse in the roasting tin and cook for 40–50 minutes, basting occasionally.

3   Five minutes before the end of the cooking time, turn the birds upright to allow the skin to brown.

4   Make a good, dark gravy by adding the flour and stock to the roasting tin.

Suggested accompaniment: Matchstick potatoes (or game chips, as they are better known), green beans, bread sauce and rowan or quince jelly.

Roast Grouse à la Rob Roy

(This recipe was given to me by Christina Stewart)

Serves 2   Cooking time: approx. 1 hour

1 brace grouse
100g/4oz butter
salt and pepper
lemon juice
100g/4oz streaky bacon
sprigs of heather
flour

Pre-heat oven to 180°C/350°F/Gas Mark 4

---

1   Truss the birds in the usual way. Into each bird put 50g/2oz butter which has been seasoned with salt, pepper and a little lemon juice.

---

2   Wrap the grouse in strips of streaky bacon and a few sprigs of heather and enclose in foil. Roast for approximately 1 hour or until tender.

---

3   Boil the livers from the birds and, when cooked, mince them finely.

---

4   Ten minutes before serving, remove the bacon and heather from the grouse. Dust each bird with seasoned flour and return to the oven, uncovered, to brown.

---

5   Spread the liver on to slices of toast and sit the birds on these. Pop them into the oven to keep warm while you make the gravy, which should be thin, adding only gravy salt, seasoning and water.

To serve: Serve the birds on their toasts.

Suggested accompaniment: Rowan jelly, pickled peaches, fried breadcrumbs, mushrooms and chipped potatoes (game chips) and gravy.

Marinated Grouse

Serves 4   Marinating time: 12 hours   Cooking time: 50–60 minutes

1 brace grouse

For the marinade:
150ml/¼ pint olive oil
150ml/¼ pint red wine
squeeze of lemon juice
3 crushed juniper berries
salt and pepper

The marinade:

1   Split the grouse in half along the breastbone.

2   Mix all the marinade ingredients together thoroughly and pour this over the birds. Leave this to stand for at least 12 hours, turning the joints occasionally.

The cooking:

Pre-heat oven to 170°C/325°F/Gas Mark 3

1   Remove the grouse from the marinade and place them on a rack in a roasting tin. Spoon a little of the marinade over each half.

2   Cover the tin with foil and place in the oven for 40 minutes.

3   Remove the foil from the tin. Baste the birds and return them to the oven for a further 10–15 minutes.

4   Put the grouse aside to keep warm and make a thin gravy with the pan juices.

To serve: Garnish the grouse with thin lemon slices and serve with the gravy.

Suggested accompaniment: New potatoes, braised celery and baked onions.

Grouse Breast in Cream

This recipe for the breast of grouse in cream may seem unforgivably wasteful but the end result is quite delicious and there are many ways to use up the left-over pieces.

Cooking time: 10–15 minutes

1 grouse per person
flour to coat
5ml/1 teaspoon mixed herbs
salt and pepper
butter
cream

---

1   Remove the breasts from the bone carefully with a sharp knife and place on a wooden chopping board or secure surface. Beat them flat with a steak hammer (meat tenderiser) and cut the breasts lengthwise into 1 inch strips.

---

2   Roll the breasts up tightly and coat them in flour which has been seasoned with herbs, salt and pepper.

---

3   Melt the butter in a frying pan and gently cook the grouse until it is golden brown (10–15 minutes).

---

4   Pour the cream on top and heat thoroughly over a gentle heat.

Suggested accompaniment: Plain boiled potatoes or sauté potatoes, asparagus, buttered broccoli, red cabbage.

Grilled Grouse

Serves 4   Cooking time: 15 minutes

1 brace very young grouse
salt and pepper
butter, melted

---

1   Split the birds in half along the breastbone.

---

2   Place the birds in the grill pan and brush them liberally with the melted butter. Season well with salt and pepper.

---

3   Place the pan under a very hot grill and cook the joints for 6 or 7 minutes each side. Brush with more butter as required.

To serve: Serve immediately topped with a little melted butter and the pan juices.

Suggested accompaniment: New potatoes and leaf spinach.

Braised Grouse

Serves 4   Cooking time: 1½–2 hours

1 brace grouse
butter
2 onions, chopped
3 stalks celery, chopped
2 cooking apples, peeled and
    diced
50g/2oz raisins
game stock
salt and pepper

Pre-heat oven to 150°C/300°F/Gas Mark 2

1   Halve each grouse.

2   Melt a little butter gently in a frying pan and brown the birds.

3   Place the onions, celery, apples and raisins in layers in a deep casserole. Place the joints in the casserole and just cover with game stock. Season with salt and pepper.

4   Cover and put the casserole in the oven to cook for 1½–2 hours. More stock may be added if required.

To serve: Braised grouse should be served straight from the casserole.

Suggested accompaniment: Sweet potatoes and peas.

Casserole of Grouse

Serves 4   Cooking time: 1½ hours

2 brace grouse
a little bacon fat
a little butter
100g/4oz mushrooms, sliced
1 or 2 carrots, sliced
12 button onions
a few crushed juniper berries
salt and pepper
150ml/¼ pint red wine
275ml/½ pint of stock made from
*   the giblets*
30ml/2 tablespoons brandy
30ml/2 tablespoons cornflour
150ml/¼ pint double cream

Pre-heat oven to 170°C/325°F/Gas Mark 3

---

1   Melt the fat in a pan, add the grouse and brown all over. Remove the birds and put them in a casserole.

---

2   Gently cook the mushrooms in a little butter and add them along with the carrots, onions, juniper berries, salt and pepper to the casserole.

---

3   Pour the wine and the stock over the birds, cover and cook in a moderate oven for 1½ hours.

---

4   Remove the grouse, putting them aside to keep warm.

---

5   Add the brandy to the casserole along with the cornflour (which has been dissolved in a little water) and cook for a few minutes until thick.

---

6   Fold in the double cream carefully. Return the birds to the pot.

Suggested accompaniment: Game chips, buttered carrots and redcurrant jelly.

Grouse Cassoulet

Serves 6–8   Cooking time: 6 hours

1 brace grouse, jointed
350g/12oz haricot beans
700g/1½lb belly pork joint
3 garlic cloves, crushed
2 celery sticks, chopped
2 carrots, diced
1 large onion, chopped
1 sachet bouquet garni
5ml/1 teaspoon sage
salt and pepper
30ml/2 tablespoons tomato purée
5ml/1 teaspoon English mustard
225g/8oz garlic sausage, chopped

Pre-heat oven to 180°C/350°F/Gas Mark 4

---

1   Wash and soak the beans in cold water overnight.

---

2   Drain and place in the bottom of a heavy-based casserole. Add the pork joint, vegetables, herbs and seasoning to the pot. Pour over enough water to cover, and stir in the purée and the mustard.

---

3   Cover the dish and cook in the oven for 2 hours. Check during cooking that the joint is covered and, if required, top up with water.

---

4   Reduce the heat to 150°C/300°F/Gas Mark 2 and continue to cook for a further 2½ hours. Check frequently and add more water as required.

---

5   Remove the pork from the casserole and set aside. Add the grouse and the sausage and make sure they are well covered by the other ingredients before returning the pork to the dish. Cover and return the casserole to the oven for a further 1¼ hours.

---

6   Remove the lid from the casserole and continue cooking for 20 minutes.

To serve: The cassoulet should be served from the casserole.

Suggested accompaniment: Garlic bread.

Barbecued Grouse I

Serves 4   Cooking time: 10–15 minutes

As eating out-of-doors seems to increase our appetites, I would allow a whole grouse per person.

2 brace young grouse, halved
1 clove garlic, crushed
25g/1oz butter
oil

1   Mix the garlic into the butter and, taking a teaspoonful at a time, carefully push it under the skin of the grouse breasts.

2   Brush the grouse liberally with oil and place them on the hot barbecue. Turn occasionally during cooking and, to prevent the birds from drying out, brush with oil as required. Cook for about 10–15 minutes.

To serve: Serve the grouse as it is ready, with a selection of salads, pickles and sauces.

Barbecued Grouse II

Serves 8   Resting time: 4 hours   Cooking time: 25–30 minutes

2 brace young grouse, halved
425g/15oz tin peach slices in
   syrup
30ml/2 tablespoons tomato purée
5ml/1 teaspoon English mustard
1 green pepper cut into strips
1 red pepper cut into strips

1 Drain the peaches from the syrup and set aside.

2 Mix the syrup with the purée and mustard and pour this over the grouse. Leave to stand for 4 hours. Baste frequently.

3 Cut 8 strips of foil and oil well. Place the peach slices and strips of pepper in the middle of four of them.

4 Take the grouse halves from the syrup and place them on top of the fruit and peppers. Spoon over a little of the syrup mixture.

5 Using the remaining foil strips as lids, tightly wrap the foil to form parcels and cook on the barbecue for 25–30 minutes. Turn once.

To serve: Unwrap the foil carefully and serve immediately.

Suggested accompaniment: New potatoes and courgettes halved and stuffed with bacon and tomato. These can also be cooked in foil parcels on the barbecue.

Layered Grouse

Serves 4   Cooking time: 30 minutes

As this dish is cooked upside-down then turned out, use a large, round, straight-edged or pudding-shaped dish.

450g/1lb cooked grouse, sliced
butter
2 large onions, sliced into rings
15ml/1 tablespoon hot curry
   powder
425g/15oz tin tomatoes, drained
   and chopped
100g/4oz mature cheddar cheese,
   grated
4 hard-boiled eggs, sliced
425ml/3/4 pint white sauce
225g/8oz rice, boiled

Pre-heat oven to 180°C/350°F/Gas Mark 4

---

1   Melt the butter over a low heat. Add the onions and cook until transparent. Sprinkle over the curry powder and mix well. Remove from the heat.

---

2   Spread half the tomatoes over the bottom of a large dish. Using half the quantities listed above, follow this with layers of grouse, onions, cheese and eggs.

---

3   Make a second layer of tomatoes, grouse, onions, cheese and eggs. Pour the white sauce over and top with the boiled rice.

---

4   Cover the dish with foil and reheat in the oven for 30 minutes.

To serve: Turn the layered grouse out on to a serving dish and serve immediately.

Quick Salmi of Grouse

Serves 4   Cooking time: 20 minutes

450g/1lb cooked grouse
50g/2oz butter
1 stick celery, chopped
1 onion, chopped
1 carrot, diced
1 clove garlic, crushed
100g/4oz mushrooms, sliced
15ml/1 tablespoon flour
275ml/½ pint good game stock
70ml/2½fl oz red wine
juice of ½ lemon
30ml/2 tablespoons tomato purée
salt and pepper
parsley and croûtons to garnish

---

1   Melt the butter in a pan and add the vegetables. Simmer gently for 10 minutes or until the vegetables are soft, stirring occasionally.

---

2   Stir in the flour to make a soft roux and gradually pour in the stock, stirring continually.

---

3   Add the wine, lemon juice and the purée and season with salt and pepper. Simmer for 10 minutes.

---

4   Cut up the grouse and add this to the sauce. Heat through gently.

To serve: Transfer the salmi to a serving dish, sprinkle with parsley and surround with croûtons.

Suggested accompaniment: Plain boiled rice.

CHAPTER 3
WOODPIGEON

Of the five species of pigeon to be found in Great Britain, the woodpigeon is the most common. Its population has swollen since the nineteenth century as a result of increased arable farming and the revival of forestry: intensive cropping of farmland has provided the pigeons with an enormous larder full of food. Following their colonisation of Shetland in 1940 they have now bred in every county of Great Britain.

It has been suggested that the total population of woodpigeon can devour 355 tonnes/350 tons of food per week at certain times of the year, which represents seven thousand sacks of grain; so you can appreciate the great damage that these birds inflict. They cost the country millions in lost agricultural revenue each year and are the farmer's enemy and an agricultural pest. But they are also considered by many shooting people to be one of the most sporting birds and they do make very fine eating. Every cloud has a silver lining!

The movements of woodpigeon are both complex and uncertain. Continental birds may migrate to England in winter and some Scottish birds may move south at this time. It is believed that some West Country birds may winter in Ireland. Continental pigeons that invade our shores are slightly smaller and darker than our native population.

The feeding patterns of pigeon vary with the seasons. Late summer sees pigeon feeding on peas, beans and oil-seed rape; at harvest time the birds fill themselves with ripe grain, and in early November they will be feeding on beech mast and acorns. Then they turn their attention to the farmer's green crops and, with large numbers concentrated into a small area, this is when the greatest damage can be done. If there is a fall of snow, pigeon will search out any turnip tops that are still showing but, if the hard weather is prolonged, the birds will starve.

Squab pie or pudding is a great favourite with many country people. Squabs are the young pigeons recognisable by the fact that they do not display the familiar neck ring until they are four months old. The squab's plumage is otherwise similar to the adult bird's, being predominantly grey on the back and paler underneath with a pinkish tinge to the breast, a metallic, greenish-purple gloss on the side of the neck and very distinctive, broad white bands across its wings.

If you can be bothered with plucking it, the woodpigeon makes a good roast, but as there is so little meat on the legs I skin them when possible and cut out the breasts. They do not require hanging and should be drawn and the crops carefully removed as soon as possible.

Pigeon Terrine

(This recipe was given to me by Karen Sommer)

Serves 12   Cooking time: 2½–3 hours

6 pigeon breasts
1 large onion
3 cloves garlic
salt and freshly ground black
*   pepper*
50g/2oz butter
175g/6oz minced pork
100g/4oz minced ox liver
100g/4oz minced chicken liver
100g/4oz streaky bacon
2 measures brandy
2 glasses red wine or port
150ml/¼ pint cream

Pre-heat oven to 150°C/300°F/Gas Mark 2

1   Finely dice the pigeon breasts and the onion.

2   Crush the garlic cloves and mix with a little salt.

3   Melt the butter in a deep, heavy-based pan or casserole. Fry the onion gently until golden and add the chicken liver, ox liver, pork, streaky bacon, pigeon and garlic. Mix well. Continue to cook over a low heat for an hour, stirring thoroughly every few minutes.

4   Pour the wine, brandy and cream over the top. Season well and transfer to the terrine. Half fill a roasting tin with water and allow the terrine to stand in this. Cook in oven for 1½–2 hours. Allow to cool and set.

To serve: This dish improves with keeping. I would suggest it be made 1 or 2 days in advance.

Suggested accompaniment: Side salad and toast or on its own with a twist of lemon.

Pot-Roasted Pigeon

Serves 4   Cooking time: 2 hours

2 pigeons
100g/4oz fresh white
  breadcrumbs
25g/1oz shredded suet
5ml/1 teaspoon mint, chopped
5ml/1 teaspoon tarragon,
  chopped
5ml/1 teaspoon parsley, chopped
grated rind ½ orange
salt and pepper
1 egg, beaten
butter

Pre-heat oven to 150°C/300°F/Gas Mark 2

---

1   Mix together the breadcrumbs, suet, herbs and orange rind. Season with salt and pepper and bind with the beaten egg. Stuff the pigeons with this mixture.

---

2   Place the birds in a chicken brick or heavy-based casserole. Dot with butter. Season and cover with a tight-fitting lid.

---

3   Cook the birds in the oven for 2 hours.

---

4   Lift the birds from the dish and keep warm. Make a gravy with the pan juices.

To serve: Split the birds in half and serve with the gravy.

Suggested accompaniment: Roast potatoes, peas, carrots and mint jelly.

Pigeon à la Provencale

Serves 4   Marinating time: 10 hours   Cooking time: 45 minutes

4 young pigeons
10ml/2 teaspoons fresh parsley,
  chopped
10ml/2 teaspoons fresh rosemary,
  chopped
10ml/2 teaspoons fresh
  marjoram, chopped
2 garlic cloves, crushed
45ml/3 tablespoons olive oil
10ml/1 teaspoon grainy mustard
salt and pepper
15fl oz/¾ pint red wine

---

1   Carefully mix together the herbs, oil, garlic and mustard. Season with salt and pepper.

---

2   Place the pigeons on a large dish and spoon this mixture over them. Leave to stand in a cool place overnight. Baste once or twice if possible.

Pre-heat oven to 180°C/350°F/Gas Mark 4

---

3   Pour the wine over and roast the pigeons for 45 minutes.

Suggested accompaniment: Ratatouille and baked potatoes.

Casseroled Woodpigeon

Serves 2   Cooking time: 2 hours

2 pigeons
some flour
pinch mixed herbs
salt and pepper
a little butter
1 onion
100g/4oz mushrooms
½ red pepper cut into thin strips
2 sticks celery
1 clove garlic
150ml/¼ pint wine
stock made from the giblets

Pre-heat oven to 170°C/325°F/Gas Mark 3

---

1   Coat the birds with flour which has been seasoned with the herbs, salt and pepper.

---

2   Melt the butter gently in a frying pan and slowly brown the birds all over. Transfer them to a casserole.

---

3   Fry the onion, mushrooms, red pepper, celery and crushed garlic for 2–3 minutes, then add them to the dish.

---

4   Completely cover the birds with the wine and stock and cook for about 2 hours.

To serve: Remove the casserole from the oven. If necessary the sauce can be topped up with a little more stock or wine or, if preferred, some cream. Reheat gently on top of the stove.

Suggested accompaniment: Brussels sprouts halved and gently fried in butter, boiled and mashed carrots and jacket potatoes.

Spiced Pigeon Stew

Serves 4   Resting time: 2 hours   Cooking time: 1 hour

4 pigeons, halved
5ml/1 teaspoon garlic salt
5ml/1 teaspoon ground ginger
5ml/1 teaspoon ground cinnamon
2.5ml/½ teaspoon cayenne
  pepper
2.5ml/½ teaspoon salt
30ml/2 tablespoons oil
2 onions, finely chopped
1 stick celery, chopped
1 carrot, diced
1 medium potato, peeled and
  cubed

400g/14oz tin tomatoes
1 red pepper, cut into strips
400g/14oz tin chick peas
150ml/¼ pint natural yoghurt

1   Brush each pigeon half with a little oil. Carefully mix together all the spices and sprinkle them over the pigeons. Leave to stand for 2 hours.

2   Pour a little oil into a pan and, over a low heat, gently cook the onion, celery, carrot and potato for a few minutes, stirring continually. Remove the vegetables from the pan and put them aside.

3   Pour a little more oil into the pan. Add the pigeons and gently brown them on all sides.

4   Return the cooked vegetables with the tomatoes and red pepper to the pot. Cover and simmer for 40 minutes. Check occasionally and, if required, a little water may be added to keep the dish from drying out.

5   Stir in the chick peas. Cover and continue to cook for a further 15 minutes.

6   Remove the pot from the heat and carefully stir in the yoghurt. Reheat very gently.

To serve: Taste for seasoning and add a little salt or sugar as required. Serve the dish piping hot.

Suggested accompaniment: A little plain, boiled rice may be served, but as the dish is quite filling a plain green salad and perhaps a little French loaf would be sufficient.

Pigeon with Apricots and Dates

Serves 4   Cooking time: 1 hour

2 pigeons, halved
3 apricots, peeled and stoned
12 dates, halved and stoned
150ml/¼ pint red wine
4 bacon rashers

Pre-heat oven to 180°C/350°F/Gas Mark 4

1   Chop the apricots and place them in the bottom of a casserole. Add the dates. Pour over half the wine and stir.

2   Place a rasher of bacon around each pigeon half and place on top of the fruit. Pour over the remaining wine. Cover and cook in the oven for 1 hour.

To serve: Place the pigeons on a platter and spoon the fruit and wine over the top.

Suggested accompaniment: Baby onions and riced potatoes or boiled rice.

Pigeons with Cashews and Cabbage

Serves 4   Cooking time: 1 hour

4 pigeons
butter
1 large onion, chopped
1 clove garlic, crushed
450g/1lb savoy cabbage,
   shredded
175g/6oz cashew nuts
salt and pepper
275ml/½ pint stock

Pre-heat oven to 170°C/325°F/Gas Mark 3

---

1   Melt a little butter in a large, flame-proof casserole and gently cook the onion and garlic for 3–4 minutes.

---

2   Add the cabbage and the nuts and, stirring continually, cook for a further 2 minutes. Do not allow the cabbage to become brown as this will spoil the flavour. Season with salt and pepper.

---

3   Pour in the stock and mix well.

---

4   Place the pigeons on the top of the vegetables. Dot with a little butter. Cover and cook in the oven for 1 hour.

To serve: The pigeons should be served on a bed of cabbage.

Suggested accompaniment: Jacket potatoes and baked tomatoes.

Breasts of Pigeon
with Apples and Grapes

Serves 4   Marinating time: 8 hours   Cooking time: 1 hour 20 minutes

8 pigeon breasts
butter
450g/1lb cooking apples, peeled
    and chopped
225g/8oz black grapes, skinned
    and deseeded
150ml/¼ pint single cream

For the marinade:
275ml/½ pint red wine
5ml/1 teaspoon French mustard
15ml/1 tablespoon dark brown
    sugar

---

1   Mix the marinade ingredients together and pour over the pigeons. Leave to steep overnight.

    Pre-heat oven to 170°C/325°F/Gas Mark 3

---

2   Drain the breasts, retaining the marinade.

---

3   Melt a little butter over a low heat in a flame-proof casserole and gently sear the pigeons. Add the marinade and the apples to the dish. Cover and cook in the oven for 1 hour.

---

4   Stir in the grapes, cover and return the dish to the oven for a further 20 minutes.

---

5   Carefully pour in the cream and reheat over a low heat, stirring occasionally.

To serve: This should be served straight from the dish.

Suggested accompaniment: Noisette potatoes and French beans.

Pigeon with Haricot Beans·

Serves 4   Soaking time: 12 hours   Cooking time: 1½–2 hours

8 pigeon breasts
225g/8oz haricot beans
100g/4oz salt pork
25g/1oz butter
1 onion, chopped
5ml/1 teaspoon mixed herbs
salt and pepper
2 carrots, sliced
425ml/¾ pint stock

1 Soak the haricot beans in cold water for 12 hours.

   Pre-heat oven to 170°C/325°F/Gas Mark 3

2 Cut the pork and pigeon into small cubes.

3 Melt the butter in a flame-proof casserole and gently cook the onion, pork
   and pigeon for 8–10 minutes.

4 Add the mixed herbs, salt and pepper, rinsed beans, carrot and stock.
   Cover and cook in the oven for 1½–2 hours.

Suggested accompaniment: Braised leeks and boiled potatoes.

Pigeons with Liver

Serves 4   Cooking time: 1½ hours

4 pigeon breasts, diced
flour
5ml/1 teaspoon mixed herbs
salt and pepper
225g/8oz lamb's liver, diced
butter
100g/4oz smoked bacon, chopped
1 large onion, chopped
75ml/3fl oz red wine
75ml/3fl oz single cream
    (optional)

Pre-heat oven to 150°C/300°F/Gas Mark 2

---

1   Mix the flour with the herbs, season with salt and pepper and use to coat the pigeon and the liver.

---

2   Melt a little butter over a low heat in a heavy-based casserole. Gently fry the bacon until the fat runs. Remove the bacon from the pan.

---

3   Add the pigeon and liver to the pan and brown gently. Return the bacon along with the onion and, stirring well, pour in enough water to just cover. Stir in the wine. Reheat slowly, stirring continuously.

---

4   Cover the casserole and cook in the oven for 1½ hours. Check during cooking and add a little more water or wine to cover.

---

5   Pour in the cream and serve immediately.

Suggested accompaniment: Button mushrooms, braised celery and sautéd potatoes.

Pigeons in Pastry Parcels

Serves 6   Resting time: 4 hours   Cooking time: 30–40 minutes

6 pigeon breasts
French mustard
shortcrust pastry
dark brown sugar
225g/8oz mushrooms, sliced
   thinly

1   Spread the pigeon breasts with enough French mustard to cover completely.
    Allow to stand for at least 4 hours.

    Pre-heat oven to 190°C/375°F/Gas Mark 5

2   Roll out the pastry on a floured board and cut into 6 large squares.

3   Lightly coat the breasts with dark brown sugar.

4   Place the pigeons in the middle of each pastry square and top with sliced
    mushrooms.

5   Draw the pastry upwards to form the shape of a pasty. Trim and seal well.
    Brush the tops with a little milk. Place on a baking sheet and cook in the
    oven for 30–40 minutes.

To serve: Serve the parcels piping hot.

Suggested accompaniment: Hot pickled red cabbage or sauerkraut,
sweetcorn in yoghurt and jacket potatoes.

Lazy Pigeons with Rich Herby Suet Crust

Serves 6   Cooking time: 1 hour 25 minutes

6 pigeons (12 breasts)
butter
225g/8oz bacon
flour
2 large onions, ringed
225g/8oz mushrooms, whole
bouquet garni
2 bay leaves
275ml/½ pint stock
275ml/½ pint cider
salt and pepper

For the suet crust:
175g/6oz self-raising flour
75g/3oz shredded suet
5ml/1 teaspoon chopped, fresh
   parsley
5ml/1 teaspoon mixed herbs
2 eggs, beaten
salt and pepper
a little milk to bind (if necessary)

Pre-heat oven to 180°C/350°F/Gas Mark 4

---

1   Melt the butter in a large frying pan, taking care not to overheat. Dice the bacon and cook until fairly crisp. Remove the bacon from the pan and put to the side.

2   Coat the pigeon breasts with the seasoned flour and brown them gently.

3   Put the breasts into a casserole dish with the bacon, onion rings, mushrooms, bouquet garni, bay leaves, stock and cider, and season with salt and pepper. Cover and cook in the oven for 45 minutes.

4   Check the casserole at this stage and, if it needs thickening, a little cornflour mixed to a paste may be added. Return the dish to the oven and continue cooking for a further 20 minutes, along with the suet crust.

The suet crust:

1 Place all the dry ingredients in a bowl, including the parsley, and mix well. Gradually stir in the eggs and milk if necessary until it is well mixed.

2 Roll the dough out roughly on a floured board to 5mm/¼in thickness.

3 Take 30ml/2 tablespoons gravy from the casserole to cover the bottom of a flan dish and place the suet crust on top. Put this in the oven when you are returning the casserole and cook for 20 minutes or until well risen and golden brown.

Suggested accompaniment: Boiled potatoes and braised celery.

Pigeon Stew with Herby Dough Balls

Serves 6   Cooking time: 2 hours 15 minutes

3 pigeon breasts, cut into chunks
15ml/1 tablespoon flour
5ml/1 teaspoon mixed herbs
salt and pepper
15ml/1 tablespoon oil
700g/1½ lb good stewing steak,
*   cut into chunks*
2 medium onions, chopped
2 carrots, diced
2 celery sticks, chopped
100g/4oz turnip, diced
275ml/½ pint game or beef stock
150ml/¼ pint red wine

For the dough balls:
100g/4oz self-raising flour
50g/2oz shredded suet
5ml/1 teaspoon mixed herbs
15ml/1 tablespoon parsley,
*   freshly chopped*
pinch salt
water – surprisingly little

Pre-heat oven to 150°C/300°F/Gas Mark 2

1   Mix together the flour and the herbs, season with salt and pepper.

2   Heat the oil in a large, flame-proof casserole, coat the meat and pigeon pieces with the seasoned flour and brown them lightly in the oil.

3   Add the vegetables and, stirring continually, gradually pour in the stock and the wine.

4   Cover and cook in the oven for 2 hours 15 minutes. Check occasionally and add more stock if required.

The dough balls:

1 Sift the flour. Stir the suet, herbs and salt into the flour, mixing well. Then add enough cold water to make a firm dough.

2 Divide the mixture into 12 and with floured hands (to prevent webbed fingers!) roll each portion into a ball.

3 When the stew has been cooking for 1½ hours, place the dough balls on the top of the stew, cover and return to the oven for 25 minutes. (As the dough balls require a fair amount of liquid in which to cook, make sure that the stew does not dry out by adding more stock if required. However the stew should be hot before adding the dough.)

4 Remove the lid and continue cooking for a further 10–15 minutes or until the dough balls are golden brown.

To serve: Serve this straight from the casserole.

Suggested accompaniment: Mashed potatoes and roasted parsnips.

Pigeon Pudding

Serves 6–8   Resting time: 2–3 hours   Cooking time: 4 hours

4 pigeon breasts, cubed
450g/1lb stewing steak, cubed
225g/8oz bacon, chopped
100g/4oz mushrooms, sliced
grated rind 1 orange
1 medium onion, chopped
5ml/1 teaspoon mixed herbs
salt and pepper
150ml/¼ pint red wine
Suet crust pastry – enough to line
   and cover a 1 litre/2 pint
   pudding basin

---

1   Mix together all the ingredients (except the pastry!) and allow to stand for
     2–3 hours.

---

2   Line the bottom and sides of the pudding basin with the suet crust, reserving
     enough to make a lid and carefully spoon the pigeon and steak mixture into
     the lined basin.

---

3   Pour water to within 1cm/½in of the top of the mixture (too much water will
     make the crust soggy). Cover with the suet crust lid.

---

4   Take a double thickness round of waxed or greased, greaseproof paper.
     Make a good sized pleat in the paper and cover the pudding. Cover with a
     piece of muslin and secure well with string.

---

5   Place the pudding in a large pan of boiling water. The water should come no
     higher than half-way up the basin.

---

6   Put the lid firmly on the pan and gently boil the pudding for 4 hours. Check
     the water level occasionally to ensure that it does not dry out.

To serve: Remove the muslin and paper from the basin and carefully turn
the pudding out on to a warmed plate. Serve immediately.

Suggested accompaniment: Baked potatoes and peas, carrots in parsley
butter.

CHAPTER 4

PARTRIDGE

(1 September–1 February)

There are two principal species of partridge in Britain. These are the common or grey partridge and the French or red-legged partridge (which can be subject to a number of cross-breedings giving variations in plumage).

The partridge's main habitat is on arable or grass fields but it is found almost everywhere in Britain, except on very high ground.

The grey partridge is our native species. It has a plump, grey body and short wings, giving it a rather dumpy appearance. It has a chestnut head and horseshoe mark on its breast which is normally more pronounced on the cock but may also be present on the hen. A surer guide to the sex of the grey partridge is that whereas the hen has narrow, wavy cross-bars on her wing coverts, the cock carries blotchy markings.

The red-legged partridge is flamboyant in comparison, being slightly larger with red legs and bill, a white eyestripe and distinctive bars on its sides over a main plumage colour of olive-brown.

The red-leg was introduced to this country from France by Charles II in the seventeenth century but did not enjoy much popularity until after the Second World War, when the population of grey partridges suffered a decline. It has proved hardier than the grey, more adaptable to intensification in agriculture and more suited to rearing and release because it is less prone to wander. So, for the last few decades, it has been usual for the game cook to be presented with three times as many red-legs as greys. This is a pity as the grey certainly has the edge over the red-leg, not only as a sporting bird, but also as a dish on the table.

I hope we are about to see a reversal in the fortunes of the grey partridge breeding in the wild. Before the war practically every arable field held a covey of wild grey partridge, but they have suffered, perhaps more than any other game species, from the changing country scene with its hedge removal, prairie-style farming and heavy use of chemical sprays. Now, however, we know how the wild grey partridge's habitat should be managed and preserved, to the benefit of all wildlife. If the will is there, the countryside may once again become a fit home for these plump, chestnut birds.

To age grey partidges the most reliable method is the bursa test (*see*

Introduction). Another method, as in the case of grouse, is to examine the two outermost flight feathers on the wing. If these are pointed, then you have a young bird. However, it is important to note that until early October some of last year's birds will also have pointed feathers, so another method of ageing is needed at the start of the season. First-season birds have yellowish legs and a dark beak but older birds have a paler, grey beak and are grey-legged.

The bursa test still applies to the red-legged partridge. An alternative method is once again to examine the two outermost flight feathers on the wing, although in this case you are looking to see if they have creamy tips, which will indicate a first-season bird. This colour marking disappears with age.

A young partridge, roasted, is a great favourite but like all game species they do become tough with age. Braising slowly is a good method of cooking the older birds. As partridge has quite a delicate gamey flavour, strong-tasting additions can spoil the taste. Partridge require a short hanging time (*see* Introduction).

Partridge with Cabbage

Serves 4   Cooking time: 1½–2 hours

2 brace plump partridge
175g/6oz sliced belly pork
butter
30ml/2 level tablespoons plain
   flour
1 large onion, chopped
75g/3oz green bacon rashers, cut
   into 2.5cm/1in strips
2 sticks celery
1 fresh green cabbage (approx.
   700g/1½lb)
275ml/½ pint red wine
salt and black pepper

Pre-heat oven to 170°C/325°F/Gas Mark 3

---

1   Truss the birds. Tie the slices of belly pork securely across the partridge breasts.

---

2   Melt the butter in a large frying pan and season the flour with a little salt and freshly ground pepper.

---

3   Roll the birds in the flour and gently fry them in the butter until they are golden brown all over. Remove them from the pan and set aside.

---

4   Fry the onion, celery and the bacon until they are cooked through.

---

5   Shred the cabbage, taking care to remove the tough, outer leaves and centre stalk, and place half in a deep casserole with the fried vegetables and bacon. Add the partridges and top with the remaining cabbage.

---

6   Pour the wine over, cover and cook in the oven for 1½-2 hours. If the casserole appears to be drying out during cooking, a little more wine or stock should be added.

To serve: Arrange the vegetables and bacon on a large serving dish and place the birds on top.

Suggested accompaniments: Buttered calabrese or broccoli and jacket potatoes.

Young Roast Partridge with Mushroom and Bacon Sauce

Serves 4   Cooking time: 25–30 minutes

2 brace partridge
butter
salt and pepper
fat bacon

For the sauce:
50g/2oz butter
1 shallot, chopped
100g/4oz bacon, chopped
100g/4oz mushrooms, sliced
flour
275ml/½ pint milk

Pre-heat oven to 220°C/425°F/Gas Mark 7

---

1   With great care to avoid tearing, push small pieces of seasoned butter between the skin and breasts of the birds. Place knobs of butter inside the birds too. Brush the partridges well with butter and cover each bird with fat bacon.

---

2   Place in the oven and cook for 20 minutes. Baste occasionally.

---

3   Remove the bacon from the birds and allow to cook for a further 5–10 minutes until brown.

The sauce:

---

1   Melt the butter in a pan over a low heat. Add the shallot and the bacon and cook gently for a few minutes until they are cooked through.

---

2   Add the mushrooms and cook for 2–3 minutes, stirring occasionally.

---

3   Sprinkle in enough flour (approx. 15ml/1 tablespoon) to absorb the butter and, stirring continuously, make a good roux.

4 Gradually pour in the milk, stirring continuously until the sauce has thickened.

To serve: Split the birds in half lengthwise and serve piping hot. Pour the sauce into a dish and serve separately.

Suggested accompaniment: Creamed potatoes and broad beans.

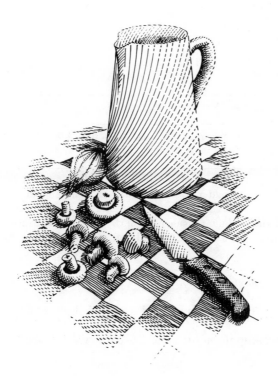

Pot-Roasted Partridge with Parsnips

Serves 4   Cooking time: 1½ hours

1 brace partridge
4 large parsnips, peeled and
halved lengthwise
2 medium onions, peeled and
sliced into rings
4 large potatoes, peeled and
sliced into rings
butter
salt and pepper

Pre-heat oven to 170°C/325°F/Gas Mark 3

1   Parboil the parsnips for 5 minutes.

2   Butter the bottom and sides of a large casserole. Place the parsnips in the dish. Dot with a little butter.

3   Place the onions on top of the parsnips and follow this layer with the potatoes. Dot with butter and season with salt and pepper.

4   Put a good knob of butter inside each bird. Brush the partridges with melted butter. Cover with a close-fitting lid and cook in the oven for 1 hour 15 minutes.

5   Remove the lid and cook for a further 10 minutes to brown the birds.

To serve: Split the birds in half and serve with the vegetables on the side.

Suggested accompaniment: Calabrese with cheese sauce.

Partridge in Tomato Sauce

Serves 4   Cooking time: 1½ hours

1 brace partridge
50g/2oz butter
1 large Spanish onion, chopped
10ml/2 teaspoons basil
1 litre/1¾ pints stock
30ml/2 tablespoons tomato purée
75ml/3fl oz double cream
salt and pepper

Pre-heat oven to 180°C/350°F/Gas Mark 4

1   Melt half the butter in a large frying pan. Add the birds and brown them all over.

2   In a large, flame-proof casserole melt the remaining butter. Stir in the onions and cook gently until they are transparent. Add the basil and season with salt and pepper.

3   Place the birds on top of the onions and pour the stock and tomatoes over.

4   Cover the dish and cook in the oven for 1½ hours.

5   Mix together the cream and purée.

6   Remove the birds from the dish and keep warm. Carefully stir in the purée and cream and gently reheat on the top of the cooker.

To serve: Split the birds in half. Spoon the sauce over.

Suggested accompaniment: Buttered noodles and a crisp green salad.

Partridge with Apple and Orange

Serves 4   Cooking time: 1½ hours

2 partridges, halved
50g/2oz butter
3 sticks celery, chopped
1 large onion, chopped
450g/1lb cooking apples, peeled
   and chopped
2 oranges, peeled and chopped
50g/2oz sultanas
150ml/¼ pint white wine
150ml/¼ pint stock
150ml/¼ pint natural yoghurt

Pre-heat oven to 170°C/325°F/Gas Mark 3

1   Melt half the butter in a frying pan. Add the birds and brown all over.

2   Melt the remaining butter in a large, flame-proof casserole. Stir in the vegetables and cook gently for 3–4 minutes. Add the fruit and stir in the wine and the stock.

3   Place the birds in the dish. Cover and cook in the oven for 1½ hours or until the birds are tender.

4   Lift the birds from the casserole and keep them warm. Pour in the yoghurt and reheat gently on top of the cooker.

To serve: Place the birds on a large platter and spoon the sauce over. Garnish with watercress.

Suggested accompaniment: Anna potatoes and a mixture of chopped, crispy bacon, peas and chopped almonds.

Partridge with Peaches

Serves 4   Marinating time: 4 hours   Cooking time: 45 minutes

2 partridges, split in half
2 fresh peaches, peeled and sliced
50g/2oz walnut halves
butter

For the marinade:
75ml/3fl oz fresh orange juice
15ml/1 tablespoon olive oil
5ml/1 teaspoon English mustard
5ml/1 teaspoon sugar

1   Mix all the marinade ingredients together and pour over the partridge joints. Leave to stand for 4 hours.

Pre-heat oven to 170°C/350°F/Gas Mark 4

2   Place the partridges and the marinade in a dish. Add the peach slices and the walnuts. Dot with butter.

3   Cover and cook in the oven for 45 minutes.

To serve: Top the partridges with the peaches and walnuts, garnish with watercress and serve.

Suggested accompaniment: Sauerkraut and Anna potatoes.

Partridge with Red Cabbage

Serves 4   Cooking time: 1 hour 15 minutes

2 partridges, halved
50g/2oz butter
1 medium onion, chopped
1 large red cabbage, roughly
  chopped
200g/8oz smoked streaky bacon,
  chopped
150ml/¼ pint red wine

Pre-heat oven to 150°C/300°F/Gas Mark 2

---

1   Melt the butter over a low heat in a large, flame-proof casserole. Add the onion and allow to cook gently for 2–3 minutes.

---

2   Stir in the cabbage and bacon. Mix well with the onion. Season with salt and pepper. Pour the wine on to the cabbage mixture.

---

3   Place the birds on top. Dot with a little butter. Cover and cook in the oven for 1 hour 15 minutes.

To serve: Spoon the cabbage on to the plate and place the partridges on top. Pour any remaining liquor over the birds.

Suggested accompaniment: Potato croquettes.

Partridge with Ginger

Serves 4 Cooking time: 45 minutes

2 partridges, halved
75g/3oz butter
10ml/2 teaspoons ginger
275ml/¹/₂ pint natural yoghurt

Pre-heat oven to 190°C/375°F/Gas Mark 5

---

1 Melt 50g/2oz butter in a frying pan over a low heat.

---

2 Put the partridges into the pan and gently brown all over. Remove from the pan and place the birds in an ovenproof dish.

---

3 Melt the remaining butter and mix the ginger into it. Pour over the partridges. Cover the dish and place in the oven for 35 minutes.

---

4 Pour the yoghurt over the birds and, leaving uncovered, return the dish to the oven for a further 10 minutes.

To serve: Serve immediately.

Suggested accompaniment: Buttered green noodles and stuffed tomatoes.

Hashed Partridges

(This recipe was given to me by Karen Sommer)

Serves 4   Cooking time: 1 hour

1 brace partridge
575ml/1 pint good stock
1 slice lean ham or bacon
1 carrot
2 onions
4 mushrooms
2 cloves
bunch sweet herbs
2.5ml/½ teaspoon Worcester
   sauce
5ml/1 teaspoon chopped capers
salt and pepper to taste

Pre-heat oven to 180°C/350°F/Gas Mark 4

1   Place a piece of greased paper over the birds and roast them for 30 minutes. Cut the birds into joints and place them in a stew pan and cover with stock.

2   Dice the ham and cut the carrot into thin rings. Slice the onions and fry them, together with the ham and carrot, in a little butter.

3   Add these to the stock, together with the mushrooms, capers, herbs and seasoning. Bring to the boil, simmer for 30 minutes, strain and skim off any fat and place the meat on a hot, shallow dish.

4   Thicken the gravy with a little flour and pour over the meat.

To serve: Serve with snippets of toast and mashed potatoes.

Partridge Pudding

Serves 4–6   Cooking time: 3½–4 hours

450g/1lb partridge, chopped
350g/12oz suet crust
175g/6oz steak, chopped
flour, seasoned with salt and
    pepper
100g/4oz mushrooms, sliced
1 small onion, chopped
5ml/1 teaspoon mixed herbs
150ml/¼ pint red wine
275ml/½ pint game stock

---

1   Roll out 225g/8oz of the suet crust to ¼in thickness. Grease a 1 litre/2 pint pudding bowl and line the bottom and sides with the suet crust.

---

2   Lightly coat the partridge and steak with flour and place in the bowl. Add the herbs, mushrooms and onion to the pudding. Pour in the wine and enough stock to just cover the meat.

---

3   Roll out the remaining suet crust and place it on top of the pudding to make a lid.

---

4   Cover the top of the pudding with a double thickness of greased paper and secure with a tightly-tied pudding cloth.

---

5   Place the pudding in a pan of boiling water to come no higher than three-quarters of the way up the basin. Cover and gently simmer for 3½–4 hours. Add more water to the pan as necessary.

To serve: Turn the pudding out on to a plate and serve piping hot.

Suggested accompaniment: Braised leeks.

CHAPTER 5

SNIPE AND WOODCOCK

Snipe and woodcock are the 'will o' the wisps' of the game shooting scene, here today, gone tomorrow. Their feeding behaviour makes them very dependent on local weather conditions; hard weather on the east coast will cause them to migrate to the milder, wetter west.

A quick glance at either species shows why they are so weather-dependent. They are both waders with long and sensitive bills which they use to probe in soft mud for earthworms, larvae and grubs. If the ground is frozen, feeding becomes impossible.

There are three species of snipe in Britain, the common, great and jack-snipe. The great and the jack-snipe are both protected.

Common or full snipe breed and live throughout Britain wherever moist, boggy conditions are to be found. They measure over 25cm/10in from the tip of the beak to the point of the tail but, because so much of this length is beak, they weigh only about 175g/6oz. They have light brown plumage striped with buff and black, the stripes on the head running from front to back. The outer of the fourteen tail feathers are tipped with white.

The woodcock is a similar but larger bird, weighing about 350g/12oz. The sportsman associates the woodcock with woodland and scrub because, as a nocturnal feeder, it rests in such areas during the day, flighting out at dusk to feed on worm-rich pastures. However, before the frosts bite hard the woodcock will also be found resting by day in long heather on the fringes of the moor.

The main plumage colour of the woodcock is rufous brown, although it may be greyish. Overlaid with buff and black stripes, this creates a near perfect camouflage among the dead leaves of a deciduous wood in winter. Unlike those of the snipe, the head stripes run from side to side, and another notable feature of the woodcock is its prominent eyes, set well back on the head to give it all-round vision. The snipe has pointed wings but the woodcock's are rounded.

Snipe and woodcock are still surrounded by an aura of mystery and folk will still argue as to whether they should be considered wildfowl or game bird. I think the description of 'hen-footed wildfowl' is rather neat in that it acknowledges their essential and different character while suggesting they are to be sought in undisturbed and often desolate surroundings.

From Norfolk to Connemara, from the Hebrides to Cornwall and the Scilly Isles, snipe and woodcock are held in the highest esteem as delightful eating, as well as wild and wonderful sport.

There is only a morsel of meat on the tiny snipe and not a great deal more on a woodcock, but what is there is absolutely delicious. Woodcock and snipe are traditionally served undrawn after hanging, but the gizzard must always be removed. To do this, make a small cut below the breastbone, just above the thigh. Use a skewer or your small finger to hook out the gizzard or use, as Crawford does, a small fishing hook from which the point and barb have been removed.

The trail becomes liquid during cooking and adds to the flavour. The head of the bird can also be left on and the bill used as a skewer when trussing, the head having been skinned and the eyes removed if desired.

For those, and I include myself, who do not care for this style of presentation, the birds can be drawn in the usual way and the head removed. Crawford says that this is sacrilege. He cannot understand why I don't mind fish heads on my plate but object to birds' heads. Neither do I, but there we are.

Roast Woodcock

Serves 1   Cooking time: 35 minutes

1 woodcock (with gizzard only
   removed)
2 slices fat bacon
stock or wine

Pre-heat oven to 180°C/350°F/Gas Mark 4

---

1   Place the bird, with the head tucked under, on a trivet in a roasting tin. Tie
the bacon slices across the back of the bird.

---

2   Cook in the oven for 25 minutes. Remove the bacon, baste well, and cook
for a further 10 minutes.

---

3   Make a thin gravy with the pan juices and some stock or wine.

Suggested accompaniment: Fried-bread triangles, roast parsnip, potatoes and warmed lemon wedges and gravy.

Roast Snipe

Serves 1   Cooking time: 25 minutes

1 snipe (with gizzard only
   removed)
1 slice fat bacon
1 small lemon wedge
stock or wine

Pre-heat oven to 180°C/350°F/Gas Mark 4

---

1   Place the snipe, with the head tucked under, on a trivet in a roasting tin. Tie the bacon rasher across the back of the bird.

---

2   Cook in the oven for 15 minutes. Remove the bacon and baste the bird well. Squeeze the juice of the lemon over the bird and return to the oven for a further 10 minutes.

---

3   Make a thin gravy with the pan juices and some stock or wine.

Suggested accompaniment: Fried-bread triangles, shallots in butter, potatoes and warmed lemon wedges.

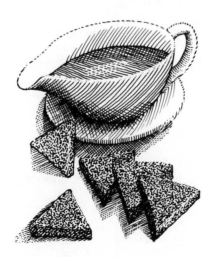

Pot-Roasted Woodcock
with Garlic

(This recipe was given to me by Jake Blackwood)

Serves 1   Cooking time: 35 minutes

1 woodcock (gizzard only
  removed)
25g/1oz butter
1 clove garlic, peeled
salt and pepper

Pre-heat oven to 180°C/350°F/Gas Mark 4

---

1   Rub a flame-proof casserole all around the inside with the peeled garlic clove. Crush the clove.

---

2   Melt the butter in the casserole and add the crushed garlic to it. Lightly brown the bird in the garlic butter. Baste well and season with salt and pepper.

---

3   Cover the dish tightly and cook in the oven for 25 minutes. Then remove the lid and continue cooking for 10 minutes.

To serve: Spoon the garlic butter over the birds and serve.

Suggested accompaniment: Toast or buttered noodles.

Stuffed Woodcock

Serves 2   Cooking time: 55 minutes

2 woodcock (with entrails
  removed)
2 shallots, finely chopped
2 rashers bacon, finely chopped
100g/4oz chicken livers, finely
  chopped
lemon juice
15ml/1 tablespoon breadcrumbs
salt and pepper

For the croûtons:
50g/2oz butter
2 slices of bread, cut into squares

Pre-heat oven to 180°C/350°F/Gas Mark 4

---

1   Mix together the shallots, bacon and chicken livers. Squeeze in a little lemon juice. Stir in the breadcrumbs. Season with salt and pepper and mix well. Stuff the birds with this mixture.

---

2   Melt the butter in a flame-proof casserole and lightly brown the birds. Baste well.

---

3   Cover with a tight-fitting lid and cook in the oven for 40 minutes. Remove the lid, baste well and cook uncovered for a further 15 minutes. Remove the birds and keep them warm.

---

4   On the top of the stove add the bread squares and fry gently until golden brown.

To serve: Place the birds on a dish and surround with the croûtons. Garnish with watercress.

Suggested accompaniment: Game chips, rowan jelly and Madeira sauce (*see* Chapter 11).

Grilled Woodcock or Snipe

Serves 1   Cooking time: 15 minutes

1 bird (gizzard only removed)
2 rashers bacon
1 slice bread
butter
lemon juice
salt and pepper

1   Wrap the bacon securely around the bird. Place a piece of bread in the grill pan.

2   Put the bird on a trivet, dot with butter and cook under a hot grill for 10 minutes. Remove the bacon and retain.

3   Continue to grill the bird for 5 minutes. Remove the innards with a spoon. Remove the bird and keep warm.

4   Chop the bacon finely and mix it with the entrails with a little lemon juice, salt and pepper and spread this on the bread. Grill for 2 minutes or until the edges of the bread are well toasted.

To serve: Serve the bird on its toast with the pan juices spooned over.

Suggested accompaniment: Fried potatoes and mushrooms.

Woodcock with Cream

Serves 2   Cooking time: 20 minutes

*2 woodcock, drawn and split in
     half*
25g/1oz butter
75ml/3fl oz brandy
75ml/3fl oz cream

Pre-heat oven to 200°C/400°F/Gas Mark 6

---

1   Melt the butter in a flame-proof casserole over a low heat. Add the birds to
the butter and lightly brown all over.

2   Cover the casserole and cook in the oven for 20 minutes.

3   On the stove add the brandy and heat through for 1–2 minutes. Pour over
the cream, heat through and serve immediately.

Suggested accompaniment: Anna potatoes and mushrooms.

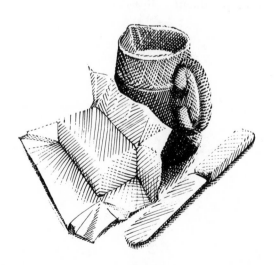

Woodcock with Whisky

Serves 2   Cooking time: 45 minutes

2 woodcock (drawn)
50g/2oz butter
salt and pepper
1 measure whisky
oil
2 slices bread cut into squares

Pre-heat oven to 200°C/400°F/Gas Mark 6

---

1   Melt the butter in a flame-proof casserole. Add the birds and lightly brown all over. Season with salt and pepper. Pour over the whisky. Cover and cook in the oven for 40 minutes.

---

2   Remove the lid and cook for a further 5 minutes.

---

3   On the stove, heat a little oil and fry the bread squares.

To serve: Place the birds on the croûtons and spoon the pot juices over. Serve immediately.

Suggested accompaniment: Roast potatoes.

Woodcock or Snipe on Toast

Serves 1   Cooking time: 25–35 minutes

1 bird (with gizzard only
   removed)
1 or 2 slices fat bacon
1 slice toast
5ml/1 teaspoon butter
lemon juice
salt and pepper

Pre-heat oven to 180°C/350°F/Gas Mark 4

1   Place the bird, with the head tucked under, on a trivet in a roasting tin. Tie
     the bacon slices (1 for snipe, 2 for woodcock) across the back of the bird.

2   Cook in the oven for 15 minutes (snipe) or 25 minutes (woodcock). Remove
     the bacon, baste well, return to the oven for a further 10 minutes.

3   Remove from the oven. Spoon out the entrails and mash them with the butter
     and a little lemon juice. Season with salt and pepper.

4   Spread the mixture on to the warm toast cut into triangles.

To serve: Place the bird on the toast and serve with pan juices spooned
over.

Suggested accompaniment: Roast parsnip, shallots in butter, potatoes,
warmed lemon wedges.

CHAPTER 6
RABBIT

Rabbits used to form part of the staple diet of many homes as they were an abundant form of relatively cheap meat. Professional warreners used to be employed to fence certain areas to keep the rabbits in and foxes out, and this brought large incomes to farmers and estates as the meat and fur of the rabbits fetched good prices compared to the expenditure involved.

In other areas, the rabbits were not managed but were nevertheless no less prolific and they were the target of every country boy and rough-shooter: even the most noble of Edwardian shots enjoyed a good day's rabbit shooting. The modern sportsman may no longer be interested in the record bags of historic slaughter, but it gives us some idea of rabbit populations to realise that 6,943 rabbits were shot by six Guns on the Blenheim estate in 1898.

Some farmers found that they made more money from the sale of rabbits than from the sale of grain; others were quite literally forced towards bankruptcy by the hungry hordes. It was probably just such a man who saw the solution to the problem in the introduction of myxomatosis to the rabbit population. He must certainly have been either quite desperate, or just plain callous to introduce such a disgusting disease. It quickly spread until the countryside was filled with blinded, staggering rabbits; their encrusted, bleeding eyes swollen closed. It was enough to put most people off eating rabbits for life.

The worst effects of the disease are long over, and it is felt that this is because many rabbits had taken to living above ground. But rabbits still give birth underground and use their burrows more in cold weather, and this can bring on a further outbreak of the disease. So if there is anything at all suspect about a rabbit's eyes – swelling, scars, bare patches or whatever – I would not eat it. Having said all this, a plump young rabbit does usually make excellent eating.

As a rabbit ages its hair greys, its ears become leathery and its claws lengthen. The soft ears of a young rabbit are easily torn and its teeth and claws are short and sharp.

Rabbit has a milder flavour than other ground game. In fact, it tastes rather like chicken and benefits from the addition of strong-tasting additives during cooking to bring out a good flavour.

Rabbit requires no hanging but should be skinned and paunched as soon as possible (*see* Introduction).

Rabbit Broth

Serves 6   Resting time: 12 hours   Cooking time: 2½–3 hours

1 rabbit, jointed
75g/3oz dried peas
50g/2oz pearl barley
50g/2oz butter beans
2 pints water
2 carrots, diced
1 large onion, chopped
1 leek, chopped
100g/4oz turnip, diced
25g/1oz rice, washed
salt and pepper

1   Cover the rabbit in cold, salted water and leave to stand overnight, and soak the peas, barley and beans in cold water overnight also.

2   Drain the rabbit and place in a large pot. Drain and rinse the pulses and add them with the other ingredients. Season well.

3   Allow to come to the boil. Reduce the heat and simmer for 2½–3 hours.

Serving suggestion: Large pieces of turnip, carrot and potatoes can be cooked in the pot at the same time for a main course of rabbit joints and vegetables.

Roast Rabbit with Sage, Onion and Orange Stuffing

Serves 4   Cooking time: 1 hour 15 minutes

1 young rabbit
100g/4oz fat bacon
flour
150ml/¼ pint cider
juice 1 orange

For the stuffing:
100g/4oz onions, finely chopped
15ml/1 tablespoon sage, chopped
1 orange rind, finely chopped
50g/2oz fresh breadcrumbs
15ml/1 tablespoon orange
*   marmalade*
25g/1oz melted butter to bind
salt and pepper

Pre-heat oven to 190°C/375°F/Gas Mark 5

---

1   Mix together the stuffing ingredients using the butter to bind it if necessary. Fill the body cavity of the rabbit with the stuffing and sew up the loose skin.

---

2   Wrap the bacon rashers around the rabbit and place the whole in a roastabag. Cook in the oven for 1 hour.

---

3   Remove the rabbit from the bag and return it to the oven for a further 15 minutes.

---

4   Make a thin gravy with the pan juices, flour, cider and orange juice.

Suggested accompaniment: Roast and boiled potatoes, French beans and roast chestnuts.

Rabbit in Red Wine with Grapes

Serves 4   Marinating time: 24 hours   Cooking time: 1½ hours

1 rabbit, jointed
150ml/¼ pint red wine
25g/1 oz flour
salt and pepper
5ml/1 teaspoon mixed herbs
25g/1oz butter
1 garlic clove, crushed
8 baby onions
2 sticks celery, finely chopped
275ml/½ pint stock
100g/4oz black grapes

---

1   Place the rabbit joints in a dish. Pour the red wine over them and leave to stand for 24 hours, turning occasionally.

    Pre-heat oven to 180°C/350°F/Gas Mark 4

---

2   Season the flour with the mixed herbs, salt and pepper.

---

3   Remove the joints from the wine and pat dry. Coat with the seasoned flour.

---

4   Melt the butter in a flame-proof casserole. Stir in the garlic. Add the rabbit and gently brown all over. Pour in the wine and stock and add the vegetables. Cover and cook in the oven for 1 hour.

---

5   Halve the grapes and remove the seeds. Add the grapes to the casserole and continue to cook for a further ½ hour.

Suggested accompaniment: Braised cabbage and buttered noodles.

Rabbit with Olives

Serves 4   Marinating time: 8 hours   Cooking time: 1½ hours

1 rabbit, jointed
150ml/¼ pint red wine
15ml/1 tablespoon oil
1 onion, chopped
100g/4oz bacon, chopped
1 green pepper, diced
5ml/1 teaspoon basil
425g/15oz tin tomatoes
15ml/1 tablespoon tomato purée
salt and pepper
100g/4oz stuffed olives

---

1   Pour the wine over the rabbit and leave to stand overnight.

   Pre-heat oven to 180°C/350°F/Gas Mark 4

---

2   Heat the oil in a flame-proof casserole. Add the onion, bacon, green pepper and basil. Stir well. Cover and cook for 5 minutes.

---

3   Remove the rabbit from the wine and add it to the casserole to brown for 1–2 minutes.

---

4   Pour the wine over the rabbit and add the tomatoes and purée. Season with salt and pepper. Cover and cook in the oven for 1 hour 15 minutes.

---

5   Add the olives to the dish and return to the oven for a further 15 minutes.

Suggested accompaniment: Buttered pasta shells and green salad.

Duchy Rabbit

Serves 4   Marinating time: 8 hours   Cooking time: 2 hours

1 rabbit, jointed
275ml/½ pint dry cider
15ml/1 tablespoon oil
1 onion, chopped
2 sticks celery, chopped
450g/1lb cooking apples, peeled
*   and chopped*
150ml/¼ pint double cream
salt and pepper

1   Place the rabbit joints in a bowl. Pour the cider over them and leave to stand overnight.

   Pre-heat oven to 170°C/325°F/Gas Mark 3

2   Heat the oil in a flame-proof casserole. Add the onions and celery and cook gently for 3–4 minutes. Stir in the apples and mix well.

3   Place the joints on top of this mixture and pour the cider over them. Season with salt and pepper. Cover tightly and cook in the oven for 2 hours, checking occasionally. Add more cider if required.

4   Take the casserole from the oven. Put the joints on a deep dish to keep warm. Place the casserole on the stove and, over a low heat, carefully pour in the cream. Gently heat through without boiling. Spoon the sauce over the joints and serve immediately.

Suggested accompaniment: Saffron rice, mushrooms and peas.

Rabbit and Smoked Pork Sausage with Chick Peas

Serves 6–8   Cooking time: 2½ hours

1 rabbit, jointed
English mustard
150ml/¼ pint cider
25g/1oz butter
1 large onion, chopped
75g/3oz smoked bacon, chopped
1 carrot, chopped
100g/4oz turnip, chopped
5ml/1 teaspoon mixed herbs
275ml/½ pint chicken stock
450g/1lb smoked pork sausage
425g/15oz tin chick peas, drained
salt and pepper

Pre-heat oven to 180°C/350°F/Gas Mark 4

---

1   Coat the joints with mustard. Place them in a large casserole. Cover and cook in the oven for 1 hour.

---

2   In a frying pan over a low heat melt the butter. Add the onion and bacon and cook gently for 5 minutes.

---

3   Stir in the carrot, turnip and mixed herbs and continue to cook for a further 5 minutes.

---

4   Add the mixture to the casserole. Pour in the stock and cider. Season with salt and pepper and cook in the oven for 45 minutes.

---

5   Cut the smoked pork sausage into 1cm/½in pieces. Add these with the chick peas to the casserole. Pour over more stock if required. Cover and cook in the oven for a further 30 minutes.

Suggested accompaniment: Potato croquettes and sweetcorn.

Paprika Rabbit

Serves 4   Marinating time: 12 hours   Cooking time: 2 hours

1 rabbit, jointed
15ml/1 tablespoon flour
10ml/2 teaspoons paprika
50g/2 oz butter
onion, finely chopped
75ml/3fl oz white wine
225g/8oz mushrooms, sliced
275ml/½ pint stock
150ml/¼ pint double cream

For the marinade:
275ml/½ pint white wine
1 onion, finely chopped
1 bay leaf
1 garlic clove, crushed

1   Mix the marinade ingredients together and pour over the rabbit. Allow to stand for 12 hours. Then remove the joints and pat dry.

2   Mix together the flour and paprika and coat the rabbit with this mixture.

3   Melt the butter over a low heat in a large stew pan. *Gently* brown the rabbit joints. Add the onion and cook for 5 minutes.

4   Pour the wine over, cover and allow to simmer for 30 minutes.

5   Add the mushrooms, mix well and pour the stock over and the strained marinade. Cover and continue to cook gently until the rabbit is tender (approx. 1½ hours).

6   Stir in the cream and carefully heat through. Serve immediately.

Suggested accompaniment: Tagliatelle verde and diced red peppers.

Pot-Roasted Rabbit

Serves 4   Cooking time: 1 hour 45 minutes

1 rabbit, jointed
2 oz lard
2 parsnips, sliced
2 carrots, sliced
1 large onion, quartered
100g/4oz turnip
salt and pepper

Pre-heat oven to 325°F/170°C/Gas Mark 3

---

1   Melt the lard in a flame-proof casserole. Add the rabbit joints and brown well. Remove the joints.

---

2   Add the vegetables to the pot and cook gently for 8–10 minutes. Return the rabbit to the pot. Season with salt and pepper. Cover with a tight-fitting lid and cook in the oven for 1½ hours.

Suggested accompaniment: Baked potatoes and cauliflower in cheese sauce.

Rabbit Stew

Serves 4   Marinating time: 8 hours   Cooking time: 2–3 hours

1 rabbit, jointed
275ml/½ pint cider
2 onions, sliced
100g/4oz ham, chopped
275ml/½ pint stock
700g/1½lb potatoes, peeled and
*   cut into chunks*
salt and pepper

1   Pour the cider over the rabbit and leave to stand for 8 hours.

2   Put the rabbit, cider, onions, ham and stock into a stew pan. Season with
salt and pepper.

3   Place the potatoes in the pan. Cover tightly and cook over a low heat for 2–3
hours until tender.

Suggested accompaniment: Mushrooms and calabrese.

Rabbit in White Sauce

(This recipe was given to me by Margie Luxmoore)

Serves 4   Cooking time: 2–2½ hours

1 rabbit, jointed
65g/2½oz butter
2 sticks celery, finely chopped
1 medium onion, finely chopped
50g/2oz flour
500ml/1 pint milk
salt and pepper
chopped parsley to garnish

Pre-heat oven to 180°C/350°F/Gas Mark 4

---

1   Place the rabbit joints in a casserole.

---

2   Melt the butter in a pan over a low heat. Add the onion and celery and cook gently until soft and transparent.

---

3   Stir in the flour and cook for 1 minute. Gradually blend in the milk. Bring to the boil, stirring until thickened. Season with salt and pepper.

---

4   Pour the sauce over the rabbit. Cover and cook in the oven for 2 hours or until tender.

To serve: Garnish with fresh, chopped parsley.

Suggested accompaniment: Boiled rice or creamed potatoes.

Rabbit with Tomatoes

Serves 4   Cooking time: 1½ hours

1 rabbit, jointed
25g/1oz butter
100g/4oz belly pork, chopped into
*   cubes*
1 garlic clove, crushed
2 onions, sliced
5ml/1 teaspoon basil
425g/15oz tin tomatoes
15ml/1 tablespoon tomato purée
5ml/1 teaspoon sugar
salt and pepper

Pre-heat oven to 170°C/325°F/Gas Mark 3

---

1   Melt the butter in a flame-proof casserole. Gently brown the pork and the rabbit joints.

---

2   Add the crushed garlic, onions, basil, and tomatoes. Simmer for 10 minutes.

---

3   Stir in the purée and the sugar. Season with salt and pepper. Cover and cook in the oven for 1½ hours.

Suggested accompaniment: Boiled rice.

Rabbit with Dough Balls

Serves 4   Resting time: 2 hours   Cooking time: 2 hours 20 minutes

1 rabbit, jointed
French mustard
1 onion, chopped
1 carrot, chopped
100g/4oz turnip, diced
salt and pepper
425ml/¾ pint stock
10ml/2 teaspoons cornflour
water

For the dough balls:
100g/4oz self-raising flour
50g/2oz shredded suet
5ml/1 teaspoon mixed herbs
salt and pepper
water

1   Coat the rabbit joints sparingly with some French mustard. Leave to stand for 2 hours.

Pre-heat oven to 170°C/325°F/Gas Mark 3

2   Place the rabbit in a large casserole. Add the vegetables, salt and pepper and pour the stock over. Cover and cook in the oven for 2 hours.

Turn up the heat to 180°C/350°F/Gas Mark 4

3   Mix the cornflour to a smooth paste with a little water and stir quickly into the casserole.

4   Mix together the dough ball ingredients and bind to a stiff dough with a little water. Divide into 8 balls and add to the dish.

5   Place the dish uncovered in the oven for a further 20 minutes until the balls are risen and golden brown.

Suggested accompaniment: Mashed potatoes and peas.

Rabbit Pie

Serves 4   Marinating time: 8 hours   Cooking time: 2–2½ hours

1 rabbit, jointed
275ml/½ pint stout
100g/4oz ham, chopped
1 onion, chopped
1 carrot, chopped
1 parsnip, chopped
50g/2oz turnip, diced
salt and pepper

For the piecrust:
225g/8oz puff pastry
milk

1   Season the joints with salt and pepper. Pour the stout over and leave to stand for 8 hours.

2   Put the rabbit and stout in a pan. Add the ham and vegetables. Cover and simmer over a low heat for 1½–2 hours, or until tender. Add a little stock if necessary.

   Pre-heat oven to 190°C/375°F/Gas Mark 5

3   Remove the rabbit and allow to cool slightly before removing the bones. Chop the meat and place in a pie dish.

4   Spoon the stout and vegetables over and mix with the rabbit.

5   Roll out the pastry and cover the pie dish. Glaze with milk and cook in the oven for 25–35 minutes or until the pastry is well risen.

Suggested accompaniment: Baked potatoes and butter beans.

Rabbit Curry

Serves 4   Cooking time: 40 minutes

450g/1lb cooked rabbit, chopped
15ml/1 tablespoon oil
1 large onion, chopped
15ml/1 tablespoon hot curry
*   powder*
425ml/¾ pint stock
50g/2oz lentils (boiled for 10
*   minutes)*
15ml/1 tablespoon lemon
*   marmalade*
25g/1oz flaked almonds
salt and pepper

1   Heat the oil in a frying pan. Add the onion and cook until golden brown. Stir in the curry powder. Cook for 1–2 minutes.

2   Add the rabbit and mix well. Gradually stir in the stock.

3   Drain the lentils and add them to the pan. Stir in the marmalade. Season with salt and pepper.

4   Cover the pan and simmer for 35–40 minutes or until thickened. Stir in the almond flakes and serve.

Suggested accompaniment: Boiled or fried rice and the usual curry accompaniments.

Rabbit and Bacon Pancakes

Serves 4   Resting time (for the batter): 30 minutes   Cooking time: 20–30 minutes

225g/½lb cooked rabbit meat,
  chopped
oil
1 onion, chopped
100g/4oz bacon
15ml/2 tablespoons tomato
  ketchup
425ml/¾ pint cheese sauce
50g/2oz grated cheese

For the pancake batter:
(Sufficient for 10–12 pancakes,
  depending on tossing ability!)
100g/4oz plain flour
pinch of salt
1 egg
milk

Pre-heat oven to 180°C/350°F/Gas Mark 4

The pancakes:

1   Mix together the flour and salt. Break the egg into the flour. Add a little milk and mix well. Gradually add more milk, beating well until the batter is the consistency of single cream. Allow to stand for 30 minutes.

2   Heat a little oil in a frying pan. Pour enough batter in to thinly cover the frying pan. Cook and turn on to the other side. Remove and keep warm on a plate covered with a tea-towel. Continue this process, keeping the pan oiled, until you have 8 pancakes. (Any extra can be stored in the freezer for future use for a pudding with lemon juice and sugar, or marmalade.)

The filling:

1   Heat a little oil in a pan. Add the onion and cook for 2–3 minutes. Chop the bacon and add it to the pan. Fry gently until it is cooked.

2   Stir in the rabbit and mix well. Add the tomato ketchup, stirring until it is well mixed.

3   Place a spoonful of the mixture across the middle of the pancakes. Roll them up fairly tightly and place them in a baking dish.

4   Pour the cheese sauce over and top with grated cheese. Place in the oven and cook for 20–30 minutes.

Suggested accompaniment: Green salad and crusty French bread.

CHAPTER 7

HARE

Two principal species of hare are found in Britain; the brown or common hare, and the blue mountain or Scottish hare. There is one other species, the blue hare of Ireland.

Thankfully the hare is not affected by myxomatosis, but its fortunes and population levels still fluctuate. Hares are vegetarian and can cause damage to farm crops and young trees; they have an extremely annoying habit of nipping the leading shoots off newly-planted saplings. So when the population levels are high, they are no friend to the farmer or forester and they can also do untold damage to cottage gardens.

Brown hares, clearly distinguishable from rabbits by their greater size and longer hind legs and black-tipped ears, live a solitary life above ground on open, rolling country. The blue mountain hare is found in the hills of Scotland where it replaces the brown hare above the five hundred-foot contour and, to a lesser extent, on some high ground in England. In summer the mountain hare has a greyish-brown coat. In winter this changes to white, with a bluish tinge, except for the tips of the ears which remain black. This serves as camouflage in the snow.

A brown hare will weigh from 2.5–5.5kg/6–12lb but the blue hare is smaller, weighing only 2–3kg/5–7lb. The blue hare is stockier and more rabbit-like in appearance, lacking the brown hare's extreme length of ears and hind legs – it even tastes rather like a rabbit.

A young hare has soft ears, a smooth coat, short, sharp claws and fairly small, white teeth. An older hare has tougher ears, the coat is more wavy and its muzzle may be grizzled with white. With age the claws become long but blunted and the teeth have grown and become yellowed.

Hares should be hung, as described in the Introduction. Although young hares need not be marinated it does help to bring out the full flavour and an older hare certainly needs to be marinated to make it more tender. Both species make good eating, the brown hare having a stronger and more gamey flavour.

Hare Soup

(This recipe was kindly given to me by Margaret McTurk)

Serves 6–8   Resting time: 8 hours   Cooking time: 2 hours 45 minutes

1 hare
4 litres/7 pints water
2 onions, roughly chopped
fresh, meaty bones (or beef stock
    cubes)
3–4 grated carrots
cornflour
salt and freshly ground pepper

1   Skin and clean the hare in the normal way, retaining the blood. Wash and joint it, then soak overnight in salted water.

2   Drain off this water and place the hare in a pan with the 4 litres/7 pints water and some fresh, meaty bones, if available. (If you are using beef stock cubes, these will be added later, as described.) Bring to the boil, then lower heat and simmer for about 2 hours until the hare meat is tender.

3   Strain the mixture and return liquor to the pan. Add the grated carrot and boil for a further 30 minutes. At the same time take the hare meat off the bones, then place all the bones and the onion in another pan. Barely cover this with fresh water and boil for about 45 minutes. Then strain this into the original carrot liquor.

4   Now add the beef stock cubes if fresh bones were unavailable.

5   Thicken the liquor to the desired consistency with cornflour mixed to a smooth cream with a little cold water. Boil this mixture for 5 minutes, then remove the pan from the heat and add the strained blood. Reheat the mixture, stirring constantly until it comes to the boil. Remove immediately, as it might curdle if left to sit and boil away.

6   Cut the hare meat into pieces and add to the soup. Season with salt and pepper. Bring the mixture back to the boil and serve immediately.

Suggested accompaniment: Mashed potato served on the same plate.

Hare Terrine

Serves 8–10   Marinating time: overnight   Cooking time: 2 hours

This terrine is best stored for at least 24 hours before use.

1 hare, skinned
450g/1lb pork shoulder, finely
 chopped
450g/1lb belly pork, finely
 chopped
10ml/2 teaspoons fresh, chopped
 basil
10ml/2 teaspoons fresh, chopped
 sage
225g/8oz streaky bacon
4 bay leaves
salt and pepper

For the marinade:
150ml/¼ pint red wine
6 crushed juniper berries
3 bay leaves
15ml/1 tablespoon olive oil
2.5ml/½ teaspoon salt
2 garlic cloves, chopped

The marinade:

1   Mix together the marinade ingredients.

2   Remove the flesh from the hare with a sharp knife. Chop it finely and place
     in the marinade. Leave to stand overnight.

The terrine:
Pre-heat oven to 170°C/325°F/Gas Mark 3

1   Remove the heart and liver from the hare, clean them and chop them finely.
     Mix together with the shoulder pork and belly pork. Lift the hare pieces
     from the marinade and add to the mixture.

2   Strain the marinade and pour the liquid over the mixture. Stir in the
     chopped basil and sage. Season with salt and pepper.

3   Line the bottom and sides of a large terrine with streaky bacon, reserving 5 or 6 rashers for the top.

4   Spoon the mixture into the terrine and flatten down evenly. Lay the remaining bacon over the mixture. Place the bay leaves on top. Cover with a double thickness of greased greaseproof paper and, finally, a layer of foil.

5   Place the dish in a roasting tin with enough water to come half-way up the terrine. Cook in the oven for 1½ hours.

6   Remove the foil and papers from the terrine and continue to cook for a further 20–30 minutes until the top is browned and firm. Remove the terrine from the oven and allow to cool. Cover and store in the fridge for at least 24 hours before use.

To serve: Hare terrine can be served as a starter with toast or as a more substantial lunch or main dish, with salads and crusty bread.

Hare Brawn

Serves 8   Resting time: 2 hours   Cooking time: 1½–2 hours

1 young hare, jointed
1 young rabbit, jointed
15ml/1 tablespoon vinegar
450g/1 lb piece ham
850ml/1½ pints stock
1 onion, chopped
10ml/1 dessertspoon grated lemon
    rind
1 bayleaf
salt and pepper
cayenne pepper

1   Place the hare and rabbit joints in a large dish. Cover with water and vinegar and leave to soak for 2 hours.

2   Remove the joints from the water and place them, with the ham, in a large pan and cover with the stock. Add the onion, lemon rind and bayleaf. Season with salt and pepper. Cover the pan and simmer for 1½–2 hours or until tender.

3   Remove the joints and the ham and allow to cool slightly before removing the bones. Finely mince the hare, rabbit and ham and place in a large dish.

4   Strain the liquor and return to the stove. Boil until it has reduced by half.

5   Stir the boiled liquor into the meat. Season to taste with salt, pepper and cayenne. Mix well.

6   Press the mixture into 8 little moulds and chill well.

To serve: Turn the brawn out of the moulds on to a large platter. Garnish with parsley and bunches of watercress.

Suggested accompaniment: Green salad, Waldorf salad, pickles and crusty French bread.

Hare Soufflé

Serves 6   Cooking time: 15–20 minutes

225g/8oz cooked hare, very finely
minced
150ml/¼ pint béchamel sauce
3 egg yolks
3 egg whites, stiffly beaten
salt and pepper

Pre-heat oven to 180°C/350°F/Gas Mark 4

1   Mix together the hare and béchamel sauce. Allow to cool.

2   Stir in the egg yolks. Season with salt and pepper, mixing well.

3   Carefully fold in the beaten egg whites. Spoon the mixture into six small
    soufflé dishes and cook in the oven for 15–20 minutes until risen and golden
    brown.

To serve: Straight from the oven as a first course.

Roast Saddle of Hare

Serves 4   Marinating time: 24 hours   Cooking time: 45–50 minutes

1 saddle of hare
5ml/1 teaspoon English mustard
100g/4oz streaky bacon
flour

For the marinade:
150ml/¼ pint red wine
2 juniper berries, crushed
15ml/1 tablespoon olive oil
pepper

---

1   Mix together the marinade ingredients. Place the saddle in the marinade and leave to stand for 24 hours, turning occasionally.

Pre-heat oven to 190°C/375°F/Gas Mark 5

---

2   Remove the hare from the marinade. Spread the mustard lightly on both sides of the saddle. Cover well with bacon, place in a roasting tin and cook in the oven for 45–50 minutes.

---

3   Remove the hare from the tin and keep warm. Add a little flour to the pan, brown gently and slowly pour in the marinade to make a good gravy.

Suggested accompaniment: Boiled potatoes, sprouts, cranberry sauce, deep-fried chestnuts.

Fillets of Hare in Cream

Serves 4   Marinating time: 2 hours   Cooking time: 45 minutes

1 saddle of hare
100g/4oz bacon
25g/1oz butter
150ml/¼ pint single cream

For the marinade:
60ml/4 tablespoons lemon juice
30ml/2 tablespoons olive oil
1 garlic clove, crushed

1   Remove the fillets from the saddle with a sharp knife.

2   Mix the marinade ingredients and pour over the fillets. Leave to stand for at least 2 hours.

Pre-heat oven to 180°C/350°F/Gas Mark 4

3   Remove the fillets from the marinade. Pat dry and wrap in the bacon.

4   Melt the butter on the stove in a flame-proof dish. Add the hare and gently brown all over. Cover the dish tightly and cook in the oven for 45 minutes.

5   Return the dish to the stove and, over a very low heat, stir in the cream. Heat through gently. Serve immediately.

Suggested accompaniment: Braised onions, spinach and roast potatoes.

Jugged Hare

Serves 6   Resting time: 24 hours   Cooking time: 3½ hours

1 hare, cut into pieces
50g/2oz butter
30ml/2 tablespoons seasoned
*   flour*
575ml/1 pint dark game or beef
*   stock*
juice of ½ lemon
150ml/¼ pint port
1 large onion, sliced
100g/4oz smoked streaky bacon,
*   chopped*
15ml/1 tablespoon redcurrant
*   jelly*
4 cloves, wrapped in a muslin bag
5ml/1 teaspoon parsley
5ml/1 teaspoon thyme
1 bayleaf

For the forcemeat balls:
100g/4oz fresh breadcrumbs
25g/1oz shredded suet
10ml/2 teaspoons parsley,
*   chopped*
10ml/2 teaspoons thyme, chopped
5ml/1 teaspoon paprika
5ml/1 teaspoon sage
1 egg, beaten
salt and pepper

---

1   Soak the hare in cold, salted water for 24 hours.

    Pre-heat oven to 170°C/325°F/Gas Mark 3

---

2   Rinse the hare and pat dry.

---

3   Melt the butter in a large, flame-proof casserole. Stir in the flour to make a roux and gradually add all the stock. Bring to the boil, stirring continuously.

4 Add the lemon juice and port and stir well. Add the hare, onion, bacon, redcurrant jelly, herbs and spices.

5 Cover the dish and cook in the oven for 3 hours.

The forcemeat balls:

1 Mix all the dry ingredients together and bind with the beaten egg. Form the mixture into balls.

2 Spoon 2 tablespoons of liquid from the casserole on to a baking tray and place the balls in the liquid. Bake in the oven for 30 minutes or until golden brown.

To serve: Serve straight from the dish.

Suggested accompaniment: Braised onions and mushrooms, duchesse potatoes and minted peas.

Hare with Cream

Serves 4   Marinating time: 24 hours   Cooking time:1 hour 15 minutes

1 hare, jointed into 8 pieces
25g/1oz butter
5ml/1 teaspoon mixed herbs
8 shallots
275ml/½ pint stock
275ml/½ pint double cream

For the marinade:
150ml/¼ pint dry sherry
15ml/1 tablespoon olive oil
10ml/2 teaspoons English
   mustard
5ml/1 teaspoon Worcester sauce
15ml/1 tablespoon tomato purée

---

1   Mix the marinade ingredients together in a large bowl. Place the jointed hare in the marinade, cover and leave for at least 24 hours.

   Pre-heat oven to 170°C/325°F/Gas Mark 3

---

2   Melt the butter in a large, flame-proof casserole. Lift the hare from the marinade, place in the casserole and brown the joints gently in the butter. Add the herbs and the shallots.

---

3   Pour the stock and the marinade into the casserole. Cover and cook in the oven for 1¼ hours.

---

4   Remove the hare joints from the dish and keep warm. On the top of the stove, over a low heat, slowly add the cream, stirring continuously until warmed through.

To serve: Place the hare joints on a bed of savoury rice. Pour some of the sauce over them and garnish with watercress and asparagus tips. Hand round the remaining sauce separately.

Caledonian Hare Stew

Serves 4   Marinating time: 8 hours   Cooking time: 3 hours

1 hare, jointed
75g/3oz butter
100g/4oz bacon, chopped
2 medium onions, sliced
1 carrot, chopped
2 sticks celery, chopped
50g/2oz flour
575ml/1 pint good stock
150ml/¼ red wine
2 bayleaves
salt and pepper

For the marinade:
150ml/¼ pint red wine
2 garlic cloves, crushed
5ml/1 teaspoon mustard

1   Mix the marinade ingredients together and pour over the jointed hare. Leave to stand overnight.

2   Melt the butter in a large stew pan. Remove the hare from the marinade and brown gently in the butter. Remove from the pan.

3   Add the bacon, onions, carrot and celery to the pan and cook gently for a few minutes. Sprinkle the flour into the pan and mix well. Gradually add the stock, red wine and the marinade. Heat through and return the hare to the pan.

4   Season with salt and pepper, and the bayleaves. Cover and leave to simmer on the stove for 3 hours or until tender. Check occasionally.

Suggested accompaniment: Creamed potatoes and braised leeks.

Hare in Cider

(This recipe was given to me by Liz McGregor)

Serves 4   Cooking time: 2–2½ hours

1 large hare, jointed into 8 pieces
25g/1oz butter
15ml/1 tablespoon olive oil
50g/2oz bacon, diced
50g/2oz seasoned flour
850ml/1½ pints cider
4 small onions
2 carrots, sliced
2 sticks celery, chopped
4 long strips orange rind
good pinch thyme or marjoram

Pre-heat oven to 170°C/325°F/Gas Mark 3

1   Heat the butter and oil in a large, flame-proof casserole and gently fry the bacon.

2   Coat the hare joints liberally with the seasoned flour and brown them well in the butter. Remove from the pan.

3   Coat the rib cage, head and liver of the hare and brown well. Remove from the pan.

4   Stir in the remaining flour, brown gently and add the cider slowly. Stir continuously to make a smooth sauce.

5   Return the hare (except the liver) to the pan, along with the whole onions, carrots, celery, orange rind and herbs.

6   Cover the casserole and cook in the oven for 2–2½ hours.

To serve: Garnish each serving with small crescents of fried bread, glacé cherries (heated in a little cider) and baby onions (cooked in cider).

Suggested accompaniment: Buttered mushrooms, French beans and game chips.

Hare Curry

Serves 4   Marinating time: 12 hours   Cooking time: 1 hour

700g/1½lb hare meat, chopped
275ml/½ pint natural yoghurt
juice ½ lemon
150ml/¼ pint oil
2 onions, chopped
2 garlic cloves, crushed
15ml/1 tablespoon medium curry
    paste
4.5cm/2 inch cinnamon stick
6 cardamoms
1 large green pepper, deseeded
    and cut into strips
425g/15oz tin tomatoes
22.5ml/1½ tablespoons ribbed
    almonds

---

1   Place the hare, yoghurt and lemon juice in a large bowl. Mix well, cover and leave to stand for 12 hours.

---

2   Heat the oil in a large frying pan and add the onion and garlic. Allow to cook gently for a few minutes.

---

3   Remove the hare from the yoghurt and add it to the onion and garlic, setting the yoghurt aside. Cook over a medium heat for 5–7 minutes.

---

4   Stir the curry paste, spices, green pepper and finally the tomatoes in with the hare, mixing well after each addition. Cover and allow the curry to simmer for 30–40 minutes.

---

5   Pour in the yoghurt. Stir well and continue to cook for a further 15–20 minutes.

To serve: Spoon the curry on to a bed of saffron rice. Sprinkle the almonds over the top.

Suggested accompaniment: Pickled peaches or mango chutney.

Casserole of Hare

Serves 4   Marinating time: 8 hours   Cooking time: 2–2½ hours

1 hare, skinned and jointed into 8
  pieces

For the marinade:
1 large onion, chopped
6 peppercorns
3 bay leaves
1 sachet bouquet garni
150ml/¼ pint wine vinegar
150ml/¼ pint red wine
575ml/1 pint water

For the casserole:
flour
salt and pepper
butter
1 large onion
1 bottle sweet stout
juice ½ lemon
7.5ml/1½ teaspoons grainy
  mustard
5ml/1 teaspoon tomato purée
10ml/1 dessertspoon sugar
1 large cooking apple, peeled and
  chopped
100g/4oz mushrooms

The marinade:
Mix all the ingredients together, totally immersing the bouquet garni, and pour over the prepared hare. Leave this for at least 8 hours, turning occasionally.

The casserole:
Pre-heat oven to 180°C/350°F/Gas Mark 4

---

1   Lift the hare from the marinade and dry each piece thoroughly with kitchen towel. Coat the joints with flour seasoned with salt and pepper.

2 Melt the butter in a large pan and gently brown the meat all over. Remove the hare from the pan and place in a large casserole.

3 Strain the marinade and pour half a pint of it over the meat.

4 Chop the onion and add it to the casserole along with the bottle of stout, lemon juice, mustard, purée, sugar, cooking apple and mushrooms.

5 Place the casserole in the oven for 2 hours or until tender. (A little extra sugar may be needed, according to personal taste. If the casserole is too watery, a little cornflour mixed to a smooth paste can be added to the pot and returned to the oven for a further 15 minutes.)

Suggested accompaniment: Creamed or Anna potatoes and some buttered broccoli and carrots.

Italian Hare

Serves 4   Marinating time: 6 hours   Cooking time: approx. 1½ hours

1 young hare, jointed
15ml/1 tablespoon vinegar
hare liver

For the marinade:
1 onion, chopped
250ml/½ pint stock (made by
   boiling the liver)
250ml/½ pint red wine
1 bay leaf

For the sauce:
2 onions, cut into rings
45ml/3 tablespoons oil and 25g/
   1oz butter
25g/1oz flour
100g/4oz piece cooked ham, diced
50g/2oz raisins
25g/1oz flaked almonds
75g/3oz plain chocolate
salt and pepper

---

1   Cover the hare joints with some water to which the vinegar has been added. Leave to soak for 1 hour.

---

2   Boil the liver with enough water to make 275ml/½ pint stock.

---

3   Mix together the marinade ingredients. Remove the hare from the water, pat the joints dry and add them to the marinade. Leave to steep for 5 hours, turning occasionally. Remove the joints and dry them.

---

4   Strain the marinade and retain.

The sauce:

---

1   Cut the onions into thin rings and fry in half the oil until tender. Remove from the pan.

2 Heat the remaining oil and butter in the pan. Coat the hare joints with the flour and fry them gently until golden brown.

3 Gradually add the marinade to the pan, stirring as it comes to the boil and thickens. Add the ham and tightly cover the pan. Simmer for 1½ hours or until tender. Add more stock as necessary.

4 Stir in the onions, raisins, almonds and chocolate. Season to taste and heat through gently for 10 minutes.

5 Mash the liver finely and spread it thinly on to triangles of warm toast.

To serve: Place the hare on a large dish of buttered green noodles. Spoon the sauce over it and garnish with the toasts.

Hareburgers

Serves 4–6   Resting time: 2 hours   Cooking time: 15 minutes

450g/1lb haremeat, finely minced
450g/1lb belly pork, finely minced
1 medium onion, finely chopped
5ml/1 teaspoon French mustard
30ml/2 tablespoons tomato
*   ketchup*
salt and pepper
1 egg, beaten
oil

1   Mix together the haremeat and pork. Stir in the onion, mustard and ketchup. Season well. Cover and leave to stand for 2 hours to allow the flavours to mingle.

2   Bind the mixture with a beaten egg. Take small portions and shape into burgers.

3   Heat a little oil in a large frying pan and cook for 6–8 minutes on each side, or alternatively brush each burger with oil and cook under a hot grill until cooked through.

Suggested accompaniment: Avocado and nut salad, relishes, sesame buns and chips.

Hare and Potato Mash

Serves 6   Cooking time: 45 minutes

450g/1lb cooked hare, minced
15ml/1 tablespoon oil
1 large onion, chopped
225g/½lb bacon, chopped
100g/4oz mushrooms, sliced
15ml/1 tablespoon tomato purée
15ml/1 tablespoon Worcester
  sauce
15ml/1 tablespoon tomato
  ketchup
salt and pepper
mashed potato

Pre-heat oven to 180°C/340°F/Gas Mark 4

---

1   Heat the oil in a large frying pan. Add the onion and cook gently until it is transparent. Add the bacon and cook through.

---

2   Stir in the mushrooms and cook for 2 minutes. Add the hare, purée, Worcester sauce and ketchup. Heat through and stir to mix well. Season with salt and pepper.

---

3   Spoon this mixture into an ovenproof dish and top with mashed potato. Cook in the oven for 45 minutes or until potato is golden brown.

Suggested accompaniment: Cauliflower cheese.

CHAPTER 8

VENISON

Deerstalking is fast growing in popularity. This is largely due to the rapid expansion in the number of roe deer which creates greater opportunities for the stalker and lengthens the season of a sport that once concentrated on the red deer of the high hills. Besides the red and the roe, muntjac, Chinese water-deer and fallow may all find their way into the stalker's larder.

The bleeding, if done, and gralloching is carried out immediately after the shot has been taken. Thank goodness for that. I hear that the stomach and intestines of a red deer can alone weigh nearly 25 kilograms, or four stone!

Many of you may in fact never see a whole deer, but buy it by the joint; others, however, enjoy rather different experiences. I still remember the first time it was mentioned that there was a deer hanging in the larder. I am not sure whether I expected it to be all neatly wrapped in freezer bags, but its only covering was its skin and fur. For those faced with similar situations, let me start at the very beginning: preparing the beast for hanging.

The first thing to do is remove the head, although I personally prefer to avoid those big, sad eyes and get somebody else to carry out this part of the operation. Normally with a buck or stag this will have already been done to remove the antlers for trophy preparation. If nobody is available, and they do seem to have a habit of making themselves scarce when a doe or hind is to be butchered, cut round the neck at the base of the skull until the head is hanging by the spinal cord. This is then severed with a knife, and the head pulled away.

To remove the feet and lower limbs, cut the skin around each elbow joint, and break the joint. Be very careful, if you have to use a knife or saw to sever the joint on the hind legs, not to sever the tendon above, as this is used to hang the carcase up for skinning.

The chest should now be opened by cutting along the throat, exposing the windpipe, and continuing the cut along the chest to the stomach cavity. The breastbone is now severed. If the heart, lungs and liver have not already been removed as the stalker and his dog's perk, these should now be removed. If you are clever, the lungs and windpipe will come away in one piece, plus the other bits.

Use a saw to sever the pelvic bone so that the 'back passage' can be removed. The carcase is now ready for skinning.

With roe deer, skinning is delayed until the end of the hanging period to prevent the meat from becoming blackened and losing its moisture. Red deer are skinned at the start of the hanging period unless they are to be collected by a game dealer who prefers them to remain intact for protection during transit.

Although you will see fairly specific hanging times for deer elsewhere in this book, a little common sense goes an awful long way, and if the smell of the carcase is giving you concern the day after it has been shot in a warm summer, don't delay. There is no point in waiting for the carcase to go rotten just because you have read that a deer should be hung for a minimum of x days. Equally, you should expect to hang a roe carcase for about a week or more in cold weather, while red deer will be hung for longer; as much as two or even three weeks.

The two main points about hanging venison are to keep flies off the carcase and to choose a fairly cool and well-ventilated spot. If you are expecting to deal with quite a few deer, an ideal solution is to build a small game larder in a shed in the shape of a triangular corner cupboard. By constructing the roof and door of perforated gauze, this provides ventilation but keeps the flies out. A beam across the larder will allow you to hang the deer by its hind legs from two meat hooks. A suitable stick, wedged between the two sides of its rib cage, will keep the chest cavity ventilated. This ventilation is important. Keep the carcase away from the walls; in fact nothing should be touching it if possible.

Deer are traditionally skinned while hung from a low rafter and this is still the best way to skin red, but for roe deer I prefer to lay the carcase on a table on its back with the legs spread out.

Slit the skin on each leg where it has been severed for hanging. Insert two fingers and the knife blade between them to cut carefully toward the chest cavity for the front legs, and toward the belly cavity for the back. Your fingers are there to avoid you cutting the meat: as your knife will be sharp, make sure you don't cut your fingers either.

When peeling the skin away from the meat, always work towards the backbone. Eventually you will have a carcase with the skin attached only along the back and haunches. You could turn the carcase over, but it is probably easier to put it back on the hooks to complete the skinning. Try to pull the skin away rather than using the knife, but be careful not to tear the meat.

Now you are ready to cut up the carcase. Let us hope that it will be a roe for your first attempt because it is far less complicated.

With the carcase still hanging on the meat hooks, remove the shoulder. You will find that these are attached only by muscle, so this is a simple but carefully-executed cutting job.

Now take a saw and remove the ribs. You don't cut venison into chops. By cutting down the ribs, just outside the line of thick meat on either side of the backbone, you are preparing the saddle, one of the best cuts.

So now you have the two hindquarters hanging from their hooks, and a dangling length of backbone and meat. Cut away the neck which can be cut into cutlets and the bones, used together with the ribs, will make stock. Sever the saddle where it meets the haunches. Cut down through the haunches with a saw in order to separate them, and lift them from their hooks. There you go: two shoulders, two haunches and one saddle, all ready for the kitchen or deep-freeze.

For many stalkers the best part of the deer is the offal. Some find the liver and kidneys rather strongly flavoured and prefer them soaked overnight in preparation for a delicious breakfast. The heart makes good mince, but some feed it to their dog, together with the lungs.

For red deer, the British Deer Society produces a pamphlet of venison recipes which includes a diagram of the cuts to be taken off the carcase, but like me, you may care to present this, along with the carcase and a fistful of notes, to your friendly, neighbourhood butcher!

Having achieved all this you are now quite entitled to treat yourself to a celebration meal — if you can face it! There is little to surpass a joint of young venison, roasted and served with the trimmings. There is virtually no fat on venison and it will not disappear before your eyes when it has cooked; this does mean, however, that extra care is needed to ensure that your joint does not dry out. Most venison joints benefit from being steeped in a marinade for a day or two, especially those of the older of the species. A piece of young roe deer does not necessarily need marinating but it should either be covered in a thick flour and water paste, which helps to retain the moisture, or carefully larded.

Venison Terrine

(This recipe was given to me by Pamela Pumphrey)

Serves 4   Marinating time: 18 hours   Cooking time: 1½-2 hours

This terrine is best stored chilled for 3–4 days before use.

450g/1lb venison for stewing
1 large onion, chopped
6 peppercorns
4 cloves
150ml/¼ pint red wine
1 bay leaf
salt and pepper
350g/12oz streaky bacon
275g/10oz chicken

1   Mince the venison and place it in a bowl with the onion, peppercorns, cloves, bay leaf, seasoning and wine. Leave to steep for 18 hours.

Pre-heat oven to 170°C/325°F/Gas Mark 3

2   Line the bottom and sides of a terrine with the bacon. Finely mince the chicken and spread it on to the bacon.

3   Remove the peppercorns, bay leaf and cloves from the venison. Spread the venison in wine on to the chicken. Press down evenly and place more bacon across the top of the mixture to cover.

4   Cover the terrine with foil and place the dish in a roasting tin half-filled with water. Cook in the oven for 1½-2 hours.

5   Drain off any excess fat. Chill and store for 3–4 days before use.

Suggested accompaniment: Crusty French bread and a crisp green salad.

Potted Venison

Serves 6–8   Resting time: 1 hour   Cooking time: 2½–3 hours

Best stored for 3–4 days before eating.

1kg/2½lb piece venison
15ml/1 tablespoon oil
salt and pepper
4 juniper berries, crushed
150ml/¼ pint port
70ml/2½fl oz red wine
50g/2oz butter
clarified butter

Pre-heat oven to 150°C/300°F/Gas Mark 2

---

1   Brush the venison with oil and season with salt and pepper. Leave in a cool place for 1 hour.

---

2   Place the venison in a casserole with the juniper berries, port and red wine. Dot with the butter. Cover the dish with a double thickness of foil or waxed paper and finally tie on the lid. Cook in the oven for 2½–3 hours.

---

3   Remove the dish from the oven and allow to cool for 30 minutes.

---

4   Take out the joint and remove the bone. Chop the meat finely and place it in a liquidiser with the pan juices and blend until finely minced or chop very finely and push through a wide-meshed sieve. Adjust seasoning and add a little more wine if required.

---

5   Put the mixture into pots and allow to cool completely before sealing each with clarified butter. Store for 3–4 days before eating to allow the flavour to develop.

Suggested accompaniment: Toast or French bread sticks and salad.

Roast Venison

Serves 6–8   Resting time: 1 hour   Cooking time: 2–2 hours 15 minutes

1.8kg/4lb leg of venison
olive oil
salt and pepper
plain flour
water
a little red wine
stock from bones

1   Put a little olive oil in a bowl and stir in a good pinch of salt and a little freshly ground pepper. Brush the joint lightly with the oil and leave in a cool place for an hour.

Pre-heat the oven to 190°C/375°F/Gas Mark 5

2   Make a good stiff paste with the flour and water and completely coat the joint with this mixture. The paste must be thick or it will slide off the joint during cooking. Cook the joint for approximately 1 hour 45 minutes.

3   Take the venison out of the oven and reduce the heat to 180°C/350°F/Gas Mark 4.

4   Remove the floury coating, which will now be crisply baked, and return the joint to the oven for a further 20–30 minutes to allow it to brown slightly.

5   Allow the joint to rest by removing it from the oven and place it on a large, warmed platter, covering with foil for half an hour. The venison will keep quite hot and the flavour will be enhanced.

6   Make the gravy with stock and a little red wine.

To serve: Surround the dish with watercress and game chips or roast potatoes.

Suggested accompaniment: Lightly-boiled French beans, buttered mushrooms and baby onions. Redcurrant jelly is traditional with venison; however, quince and apple jelly is also delicious.

Braised Saddle of Venison

Serves 6–8   Marinating time: 3 days   Cooking time: 2–2½ hours

1 saddle venison
100g/4oz black eyed beans
oil
100g/4oz belly pork
2 onions, chopped
5ml/1 teaspoon mixed herbs
salt and pepper
2 carrots, chopped
water

For the marinade:
275ml/½ pint red wine
50ml/2 fl oz oil
5ml/1 teaspoon mustard
2 bayleaves

1   Mix the marinade ingredients together and steep the venison in this for 3 days. Turn occasionally.

2   Soak the beans overnight in cold water. Drain and boil for 20 minutes. Set aside.

Pre-heat oven to 170°C/325°F/Gas Mark 3

3   Remove the skin from the belly pork and cut the meat into 2.5cm/1in cubes. Heat the oil in a large casserole and gently brown the belly pork. Add the onions and mixed herbs and cook gently for 2–3 minutes.

4   Add the carrots and beans. Season with salt and pepper and barely cover with water.

5   Place the saddle on top of the vegetables. Strain the marinade and pour 60ml/4 tablespoons over the joint. Cover and cook in the oven for 2–2½ hours, adding a little of the marinade as necessary to keep the vegetables just moist.

Suggested accompaniment: Braised mushrooms and onions, croûtons and roast potatoes.

Fillet of Venison
with Redcurrant Jelly

(The following recipe was given to me by Pamela Pumphrey)

Serves 6   Cooking time: 45–60 minutes

900g/2 lb fillet of venison
100g/4oz bacon
50g/2oz butter
2 shallots, finely chopped
40g/1½ oz flour
275ml/½ pint good stock
275ml/½ pint red wine
15ml/1 tablespoon redcurrant
   jelly
12 gherkins, sliced

1   Cut the fillet into thick strips and wrap them round with bacon.

2   Melt the butter in a large pan and quickly brown the venison and shallots. Remove from the pan and put aside.

3   Add the flour to the butter, allow to brown lightly. Gradually blend in the stock and wine. Bring to the boil, stirring continuously until it has thickened and reduced.

4   Return the venison to the pan and simmer gently for 30–40 minutes until the venison is tender. Place the fillets on a dish and keep warm.

5   Add the redcurrant jelly to the sauce and stir until dissolved. Pour all but 15ml/1 tablespoon of the sauce over the venison.

6   Add the sliced gherkins to the remaining sauce. Heat through and use to garnish the fillets.

Suggested accompaniment: French beans and fried potatoes.

Venison Tenderloin

Serves 6   Marinating time: 4 hours   Cooking time: 45–50 minutes

1 venison tenderloin
150ml/¼ pint oil
150ml/¼ pint red wine
1 bay leaf
salt and pepper

For the sauce:
30ml/2 tablespoons oil
100g/4oz smoked bacon, chopped
1 onion, chopped
1 garlic clove, crushed
15ml/1 tablespoon flour
150ml/¼ pint red wine
275ml/½ pint game stock
30ml/2 tablespoons tomato purée
225g/8oz mushrooms, sliced

1   Cut the tenderloin into 6 thick steaks.

2   Mix together the oil and red wine, add the bay leaf, salt and pepper and pour this over the steaks and leave to steep for 4 hours.

   Pre-heat oven to 180°C/350°F/Gas Mark 4

3   Heat the oil in a pan and add the bacon and onion. Cook for 5 minutes over a low heat. Add the garlic and continue cooking for 2–3 minutes.

4   Sprinkle in the flour and allow to brown slightly. Gradually add the wine and the stock, stirring continuously. Stir in the purée. Bring to the boil and remove from the heat.

5   Drain the venison from the marinade and place the steaks in a shallow ovenproof dish. Place the mushrooms in the dish. Pour over the sauce. Cover and cook in the oven for 40–50 minutes.

Suggested accompaniment: Mangetout and potato croquettes.

Braised Venison Loin Chops

Serves 4   Marinating time: 4 hours   Cooking time: 1 hour

8 venison loin chops
10ml/2 teaspoons fresh basil,
chopped
2 onions, cut into rings
450g/1lb tomatoes, skinned and
sliced
50ml/2fl oz red wine
15ml/1 tablespoon oil
salt and pepper

For the marinade:
150ml/¼ pint oil
50ml/2fl oz red wine
1 garlic clove, crushed

---

1   Mix the marinade ingredients together and pour over the chops. Leave to steep for 4 hours.

Pre-heat oven to 170°C/325°F/Gas Mark 3

---

2   Drain the chops from the marinade and place in a small roasting tray. Sprinkle with salt, pepper and basil.

---

3   Put the onion rings and tomatoes on to the chops and pour the wine and oil over them. Cover the tray with foil and bake in the oven for 1 hour.

Suggested accompaniment: Courgettes, aubergine and boiled potatoes.

Braised Venison Neck Cutlets

Serves 6   Cooking time: 1½ hours

6 venison neck cutlets
15ml/1 tablespoon redcurrant
jelly
1 onion, cut into rings
1 parsnip, sliced
1 carrot, sliced
sprig of rosemary
425ml/¾ pint game stock
salt and pepper

Pre-heat oven to 170°C/325°F/Gas Mark 3

1   Spread the cutlets on both sides with a little redcurrant jelly. Place them in a shallow casserole.

2   Add the onion, parsnip, carrot and rosemary to the dish and pour over the stock. Season with salt and pepper.

3   Cover the dish and cook in the oven for 1½ hours.

Suggested accompaniment: Creamed potatoes and broccoli.

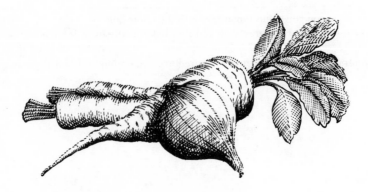

Venison Casserole

(The following recipe was given to me by Pamela Pumphrey)

Serves 6   Cooking time: 2½–3 hours

900g/2 lb venison (for stewing)
275ml/½ pint game stock
bouquet garni
thyme
1 bay leaf
1 teaspoon cornflour
225g/8oz mushrooms, sliced
½ red pepper
150ml/¼ pint red wine
salt and pepper

Pre-heat oven to 170°C/325°F/Gas Mark 3

---

1   Cut the venison into pieces and place in a casserole with 575ml/1 pint stock and the herbs. Cover and cook in the oven for 1½–2 hours.

---

2   Turn oven up to 180°C/350°F/Gas Mark 4. Remove the venison and put aside.

---

3   Mix the cornflour to a smooth paste with a little water and add to the sauce. Add the mushrooms and peppers.

---

4   Pour in the red wine, season with salt and pepper. Stir well and return the venison to the dish. Cover and cook in the oven for a further 45 minutes.

Suggested accompaniment: Red cabbage and baked potatoes.

Venison Pudding

Serves 4   Marinating time: 12 hours   Cooking time: 3½–4 hours

450g/1lb shoulder venison, cut
    into cubes
1 onion, finely chopped
5ml/1 teaspoon English mustard
125ml/4oz mushrooms, sliced
1 carrot, chopped
5ml/1 teaspoon mixed herbs
salt and pepper
150ml/¼ pint red wine

For the crust:
450g/1lb plain flour
225g/8oz shredded suet
water
pinch of salt

---

1   Place the venison, onion, mustard, mushrooms, carrot and mixed herbs in a bowl. Season with salt and pepper. Pour the wine over. Mix well and allow to stand for 12 hours.

---

2   Mix together the flour, suet and salt, and add enough water to make a stiff dough.

---

3   Roll out two-thirds of the dough and use to line the bottom and sides of a 1 litre/2 pint pudding bowl. Spoon in the venison mixture and top up with a little water, if necessary, to come within 2.5cm/1in of the pudding top. Cover with the remaining dough.

---

4   Cover the dough with a piece of pleated greaseproof or waxed paper and a pudding cloth, tied securely.

---

5   Place the pudding in a pan with sufficient water to come half-way up the bowl. Boil gently for 3½–4 hours ensuring that the pan does not boil dry.

To serve: Remove the cloth and turn the pudding out on to a serving dish.

Suggested accompaniment: Roast parsnips, peas and mashed potatoes.

Venison and Pineapple Kebabs

Serves 6   Marinating time: 18 hours   Cooking time: 20–30 minutes

900g/2lb venison
1 red pepper
1 green pepper
18 baby onions
450g/1lb mushrooms
400g/14oz can pineapple in juice,
    not *syrup*

For the marinade:
Juice from the can of pineapple
30ml/2 tablespoons red wine
275ml/½ pint sunflower oil
1 clove garlic, chopped
5ml/1 teaspoon English mustard

1   Mix all the marinade ingredients together. Cut the venison into 2.5cm/1in chunks. Put them into the marinade, cover and leave for 18 hours in the fridge.

2   Cut the peppers in half and remove the seeds. Cut each half into 3 pieces. Strain off some of the marinade and lightly simmer the onions and peppers in it for 2–3 minutes.

3   Drain the venison from the marinade and thread the meat, onions, peppers, mushrooms and pineapple chunks alternately, until the skewers are evenly filled. Brush the mushrooms liberally with oil to prevent them from drying out during cooking.

4   The kebabs can be cooked on a barbecue, under the grill or in the oven at 200°C/400°F/Gas Mark 6 for 20–30 minutes. Turn the kebabs occasionally to ensure that they are evenly cooked. A little more oil may be brushed lightly over the vegetables if they seem to be drying out.

To serve: Serve with a crisp, green salad.

Venison Curry

Serves 6   Marinating time: 18 hours   Cooking time: 1½ hours

For the marinade:
*700g/1½ lb venison, cut into
  cubes (stewing cut)*
*15ml/1 tablespoon Madras curry
  powder*
2.5ml/½ teaspoon chilli powder
1 garlic clove, crushed
juice ½ lemon
15ml/1 tablespoon oil
salt and pepper

For the cooking:
30ml/2 tablespoons oil
1 large onion, chopped
*575–850ml/1–1½ pints game
  stock*
30ml/2 tablespoons tomato purée
15ml/1 tablespoon sweet chutney

---

1   Put the venison into a bowl. Sprinkle the spices, seasoning, garlic, lemon juice and oil over the top. Mix well and leave to stand for 18 hours.

---

2   Heat the oil in a frying pan. Add the onions and cook until slightly brown.

---

3   Add the venison and spices mixture to the pan and quickly brown the meat.

---

4   Gradually add the stock, purée and chutney and heat through. Cover the pan and allow to simmer for 1¼–1½ hours until the meat is tender. Add more stock if required.

Suggested accompaniments: Boiled rice, fried banana slices, grated coconut, a sweet chutney and lemon slices.

Venison Croquettes

Serves 6   Cooking time: 10 minutes

350g/12oz cooked venison,
   minced
100g/4oz smoked bacon, minced
100g/4oz sausage meat
1 onion, finely chopped
15ml/1 tablespoon redcurrant
   jelly
5ml/1 teaspoon English mustard
salt and pepper
1 egg

For the coating:
2 eggs, beaten
flour
breadcrumbs
oil for frying

1   Mix together the venison, bacon and sausage meat. Season with salt and pepper.

2   Stir in the onion, redcurrant jelly and mustard and bind with an egg. Mix well and shape into 12 croquettes.

3   Dip each croquette into the beaten egg, lightly coat with flour, dip in egg again and finally roll in the breadcrumbs.

4   Heat some oil in a frying pan and cook the croquettes until golden brown.

Suggested accompaniment: Braised red cabbage and cheese-filled baked potatoes.

Venisonburgers

Serves 6   Cooking time: 15 minutes

350g/12oz cooked venison,
  minced
100g/4oz smoked bacon, minced
100g/4oz sausage meat
1 onion, finely chopped
15ml/1 tablespoon redcurrant
  jelly
5ml/1 teaspoon English mustard
salt and pepper
1 egg

1   Mix together the venison, bacon and sausage meat. Season with salt and pepper. Stir in the onion, redcurrant jelly and mustard and bind with an egg. Mix well.

2   Shape the venison mixture into burgers.

3   Heat a little oil in a frying pan and cook for 5–7 minutes each side. Alternatively, brush the burgers liberally with oil, and grill.

Suggested accompaniment: Pepper sauce or pizzaiola sauce (Chapter 11) and a mixed selection of vegetables.

CHAPTER 9
WILD DUCK

There are a number of species of duck which can be shot in Britain. The very keen wildfowler may bag gadwall, pintail, pochard, shoveler and tufted duck, but the majority of birds shot will be mallard, widgeon and teal. There are two others: the goldeneye, which is quite inedible (the drake is a piebald bird with a distinctive splash of white in front of his eye, on a black head), and the garganey, which is irrelevant as it is only a summer visitor and it migrates south before the first shot of the season is fired.

Of the three main species mallard should hardly need any introduction: everyone will have seen them on their local duck pond. The male or drake is a big and handsome bird with his metallic-green head, white neck-collar, light-grey body, and black and white tail.

The widgeon is a smaller bird and the great favourite of coastal wildfowlers. They are normally migrants, although some do breed in the north of Scotland. The drake has a distinctive chestnut head with a golden-yellow crown.

The teal is the smallest of European duck, being about the size and weight of a woodcock. They are tremendously popular with sportsmen, flying fast, jinking and swerving in unison within a flock. The drake has a chestnut head with a green stripe on either side, running through the eye and bordered with a creamy line.

The female ducks are harder to identify as they are all rather dowdy, brown birds. Possibly the best way to identify duck, if you are not sure, is by weight. The female mallard weighs about 1.1kg/2½lb, widgeon slightly less than 900g/2lb and the tiny teal tips the scales at only 350g/12oz.

Mallard make marvellous, succulent eating, particularly when they have been feeding on stubble in the autumn. Teal are equally good and many people prefer them to all other duck; as they are so small they make a good meal for one, with all the accompaniments. Dare I mention that one member of my family tends to leave out the accompaniments to leave room for two teal on his plate!

Widgeon make a marvellous meal when feeding on fresh marshes and grass at the start of the season but towards its end, when the duck are shot on the saltings, you must beware because they can develop a salty, almost fishy taste. To be on the safe side, soak late-season widgeon in a vinegar-water solution, and cook them with an onion inside.

The hanging of duck can cause some concern. In cold weather

hanging for up to a week will tenderise the meat, but in warm weather I would not hang the birds for more than two or three days; indeed, some would not hang them at all. Others, to be on the safe side during warmer weather, draw out the intestines through the vent using a thin nail bent into the shape of a crochet hook, and then hang their duck for a couple of days.

It must always be remembered that there is an enormous difference between wild and domesticated ducks. There is virtually no fat on the wild bird. This has a marked effect on cooking techniques.

Cream of Duck Soup with Almonds

This soup makes an unusual starter. It is quickly prepared and freezes well.

Serves 6 Cooking time: 20 minutes

225g/½lb cooked duck
50g/2oz butter
575ml/1 pint stock made from the
    duck bones (alternatively
    chicken stock can be used)
1 small onion, chopped
1 carrot, sliced
flour
1 tablespoon tomato purée
150ml/¼ pint dry sherry
salt and pepper

1   Melt the butter over a low heat. Cook the onion and carrot in it for 3–4 minutes.

2   Add the duck meat and thoroughly heat through.

3   Stir in enough flour to absorb the butter. Gradually stir in the stock, tomato purée and sherry. Season to taste with salt and pepper. Liquidise or push through a wide-meshed sieve and return to the pan to heat.

To serve: Put the soup into serving bowls, add a swirl of cream and top with a few flaked almonds.

Duck Terrine

Serves 6   Cooking time: approx. 1½ hours

Best kept chilled for 2–3 days before serving.

450g/1lb duck with bones
  removed
100g/4oz bacon
225g/8oz chicken livers
50g/2oz butter
1 garlic clove, crushed
½ orange rind, finely grated
150ml/¼ pint red wine
2 bay leaves
salt and pepper
bacon, to line terrine

Pre-heat oven to 180°C/350°F/Gas Mark 4

---

1   Cut the bacon into small strips, the duck into small pieces, and chop the chicken livers finely.

---

2   Melt the butter in a large frying pan and add the bacon. Cook gently for 2–3 minutes. Stir in the duck and the garlic and cook for 8–10 minutes over a low heat.

---

3   Add the chicken livers and orange rind. Stir until cooked through. Pour the wine over and allow to simmer for 5 minutes. Season with salt and pepper.

---

4   Pour this mixture into a liquidiser and blend to the consistency preferred, or push through a sieve.

---

5   Line the bottom and sides of a terrine with bacon strips and pour in the mixture. Place a few strips of bacon over the top of the mixture and then the bay leaves.

---

6   Place the dish on a trivet in a roasting tin half-filled with water, and cook in the oven for 1 hour. Remove the bay leaves. Allow to cool and keep chilled for 2–3 days before serving.

Suggested accompaniment: Toast or French bread and salad.

Roast Wild Duck

Serves 1   Cooking time: 1 hour

allow 1 bird per person
a little butter
strips of belly pork or streaky
*   bacon*
a little flour
salt and pepper
150ml/¼ pint red wine

Pre-heat oven to 200°C/400°F/Gas Mark 6

1   Spread the butter evenly over the birds and put a small knob in the body cavity. Place the bacon or belly pork strips across the breasts and secure with some string. Sprinkle the ducks with salt and pepper.

2   Put the birds in a roasting tin in the oven for approximately 40 minutes, basting frequently.

3   Remove the bacon and return the birds to the oven for a further 15 minutes, or until they are brown and cooked through.

4   Make the gravy, adding the wine, and season to taste.

To serve: Place the ducks on a large serving dish and garnish with orange rings and watercress.

Suggested accompaniment: Plain boiled potatoes topped with parsley, roast parsnips, buttered courgette rings and orange sauce.

Roast Duck with Nut Stuffing

Serves 12   Cooking time: approx. 2 hours

3 duck (approximately 1.8kg/4lb
  each)
15ml/1 tablespoon plain flour
225ml/8fl oz fresh orange juice
stock made from the giblets
salt and pepper

For the stuffing:
butter
1 large onion, finely chopped
250g/9oz Brazil nuts
175g/6oz almonds
250g/9oz toasted cashews
7.5ml/1½ teaspoons sage
5ml/1 teaspoon oregano
7.5ml/1½ tablespoons parsley
75g/3oz breadcrumbs
rind and juice 1 orange
1 egg, beaten
salt and pepper

Pre-heat oven to 190°C/375°F/Gas Mark 5

---

1   Soften the onion in a little butter over a low heat. Remove from the pan and put into a large mixing bowl.

---

2   Grind up the nuts so that they are fine but not powdery and add them to the onions, along with the herbs, breadcrumbs, rind and juice. Bind the mixture with an egg and season with salt and pepper.

---

3   Make sure that the duck are clean and dry before stuffing with the nut mixture. Truss the birds and weigh them. Sprinkle liberally with salt and pepper and prick all over to allow the fat to run.

---

4   Cook the duck in the oven for 20 minutes per 450g/pound, basting occasionally. Once the birds are cooked, remove to a warm plate and keep hot.

The orange gravy:

5   Pour off all the excess fat from the roasting tin. Add some flour and stir in the orange juice and duck stock. Season to taste (a little sugar can be added to the gravy if it is too tart).

Suggested accompaniment: Roast potatoes, mushroom and onion-stuffed vine leaves and thin carrot sticks. Quince and apple jelly also makes an excellent accompaniment.

Roast Teal

Serves 1   Cooking time: 30 minutes

1 teal
butter
flour

Pre-heat oven to 200°C/400°F/Gas Mark 6

1   Melt a little butter in a pan and brush this all over the teal. Sprinkle with a little flour.

2   Place the bird in a roasting bag and cook in the oven for 20 minutes. Then slit along the top of the bag and continue to cook for a further 10 minutes.

3   Make a thin gravy with the juices in the bag.

Suggested accompaniment: Fried potatoes, French beans and fried orange rings.

Stuffed Duck Breasts

Serves 4   Cooking time: approx. 40 minutes

4 duck breasts
4 thin slices Parma ham, cut in
half
4 cheese slices, cut in half
4 rashers streaky bacon
50g/2oz butter
100g/4oz pineapple chunks,
drained
8 wooden cocktail sticks for
securing
cinnamon

Pre-heat oven to 190°C/375°F/Gas Mark 5

---

1   Split the breasts in half and place a piece of ham and cheese alternately to create a sandwich effect.

---

2   Put two half-breasts together and wrap each round with a rasher of bacon. Secure well by inserting 2 cocktail sticks into each portion.

---

3   In a flame-proof dish melt the butter and very lightly brown the breasts. Cover and cook in the oven for 25 minutes.

---

4   Add the drained pineapple to the dish and sprinkle with a little cinnamon. Leave uncovered and continue to cook in the oven for a further 15 minutes.

Suggested accompaniment: Fried courgettes topped with grated cheese and roast potatoes.

Stir-Fried Roast Duck

The Chinese have so many methods of cooking duck that are quick and easy to prepare, look attractive and taste delicious that I decided to include a recipe here for stir-fried roast duck. Our increasing interest in foreign dishes has led to the supermarkets stocking a wide range of ingredients. If you do not have a 'wok', a heavy-based frying pan will do very well for this recipe.

Serves 6   Cooking time: 10–15 minutes

900g/2lb roast duck
15ml/1 tablespoon cornflour
70ml/5 tablespoons lychees
45ml/3 tablespoons lychee syrup
30ml/2 tablespoons pineapple
*   cubes*
45ml/3 tablespoons pineapple
*   syrup*
45ml/3 tablespoons soy sauce
1 carrot
1 green pepper
30ml/2 tablespoons vegetable oil

1   Remove the flesh from the duck bones and cut the meat into cubes.

2   Blend the cornflour with 45ml/3 tablespoons water and mix this together with the lychee and pineapple syrups and 15ml/1 tablespoon of the soy sauce. Cut the carrot and green pepper into small strips.

3   Heat the oil in the frying pan or wok and add the carrot and pepper. Cook for about half a minute. Add the duck and the remaining soy sauce and stir-fry for 2–3 minutes.

4   Put the lychees and pineapple chunks in the pan and continue to stir-fry for another 2 minutes. Pour the cornflour and fruit syrup mixture carefully into the pan and stir it until it thickens.

To serve: Serve this immediately with plain boiled or fried rice.

Pot-Roasted Wild Duck with Orange and Pineapple

Serves 4   Cooking time: 1½ hours

2 mallard
50g/2oz butter, melted
2 oranges
425g/15oz tin pineapple chunks
150ml/¼ pint white wine
150ml/¼ pint stock
10ml/2 teaspoons cornflour
15ml/1 tablespoon caster sugar

Pre-heat oven to 190°C/375°F/Gas Mark 5

---

1   Melt the butter in a frying pan. Truss the ducks and add them to the frying pan. Lightly brown all over.

---

2   Carefully peel and segment the oranges, removing all pith and stones. Cut the peel into thin strips and set aside. Place the segments in the bottom of a large casserole.

---

3   Drain the pineapple chunks, reserving the juice, and place them on top of the orange segments. Place the browned ducks on top of the fruits. Pour the wine, stock and half the pineapple juice over the top. Cover tightly and cook in the oven for 1½ hours.

---

4   Remove the duck and keep warm.

---

5   Mix the cornflour to a smooth paste with the remaining pineapple juice and add to the pot. Stir in the sugar and the orange rind. Bring to the boil on the stove, stirring continuously.

To serve: Split the ducks in half and spoon the sauce over them.

Suggested accompaniment: New potatoes, glazed onions and carrots.

Salmi of Wild Duck

Serves 6   Cooking time: 1 hour

2 mallard
50g/2oz butter
1 onion, finely chopped
100g/4oz streaky bacon, chopped
5ml/1 teaspoon mixed herbs
50g/2oz bacon to cover duck
425ml/¾ pint good duck stock
37g/1½oz flour
10ml/1 dessertspoon mushroom
  ketchup
150ml/¼ pint port
50g/2oz green olives
salt and pepper

Pre-heat oven to 180°C/350°F/Gas Mark 4

---

1   Melt 25g/1oz butter in a pan and lightly fry the onion and bacon. Add the mixed herbs, salt and pepper and cook for 1 minute. Pour this into the base of a flame-proof casserole.

---

2   Place the ducks on top of the onion and bacon and cover with the bacon rashers. Pour over ¼ pint duck stock. Cover and cook in the oven for 25 minutes.

---

3   Melt the remaining butter in a pan. Stir in the flour to make a roux. Gradually add the rest of the stock until thick. Boil and reduce, stirring continuously for 2–3 minutes. Reduce heat and add the mushroom ketchup, tomato purée and port.

---

4   Remove the bacon rashers from the birds. Pour off any excess fat from the ducks and add the sauce to the casserole. Cover and cook on the stove for a further 30 minutes.

---

5   Add the stoned olives and heat through gently.

Suggested accompaniment: Creamed potatoes and mushrooms.

Pot-Roasted Teal
with Apricot Stuffing

Serves 4   Cooking time: 30–40 minutes

2 teal
3 apricots
70ml/2½fl oz red wine
15ml/1 tablespoon apricot jam
2 rashers bacon
butter
salt and pepper

Pre-heat oven to 190°C/375°F/Gas Mark 5

1   Skin and chop the apricots. Place them in a pan with the wine and allow to simmer gently until tender. Stir in the apricot jam, mix well and allow to cool.

2   Mash the apricots with a fork and use to stuff the body cavities of the teal.

3   Wrap the birds with the bacon and place them in an oven dish. Dot with the butter and season with a little salt and pepper. Cover and cook in the oven for 25–35 minutes. Remove the cover and allow to cook for a further 5 minutes.

Suggested accompaniment: Creamed carrots and buttered green noodles.

Braised Duck

Serves 4–6   Cooking time: 1–1½ hours

2 mallard or 3 widgeon
50g/2oz butter
100g/4oz bacon piece cut into
*   2.5cm/1in cubes*
1 onion, cut into rings
150ml/¼ pint red wine
salt and pepper

1   Truss the birds.

2   Melt the butter in a large pan and add the bacon pieces and onion rings.
     Cook gently for 2–3 minutes. Place the birds on top of this mixture. Pour the
     wine over. Season with salt and pepper.

3   Cover with a tight-fitting lid and simmer gently on the stove for 1–1½ hours
     or until tender.

4   Place the duck on a serving dish and keep it warm. Surround with the bacon
     and onion. Make a thin gravy with the pan juices and some wine or stock.

Suggested accompaniment: A colourful mixture of vegetables cut small
and cooked in butter.

Casseroled Duck

Serves 4   Cooking time: 1½–2 hours

2 mallard, cut into halves
50g/2oz butter
25g/1oz flour
1 onion, quartered
2 parsnips, cut in half lengthwise
1 orange rind, cut into thin strips
juice of 1 orange
275ml/½ pint stock
1 bouquet garni
salt and pepper

Pre-heat oven to 170°C/325°F/Gas Mark 3

1   Melt the butter in a frying pan. Dip the duck into the flour and add to the frying pan. Gently brown all over.

2   Put the onion, parsnip and orange rind in the bottom of a large casserole. Place the duck joints on top of the vegetables. Pour the orange juice and stock over.

3   Add the bouquet garni and season with salt and pepper. Cover with a tight-fitting lid and cook in the oven for 1½–2 hours.

Suggested accompaniment: Asparagus and duchesse potatoes.

Wild Duck in Cider

Serves 4   Cooking time: 1½–2 hours

2 mallard
a little flour
salt and pepper
1 bay leaf, finely chopped
15ml/1 tablespoon olive oil
100g/4oz bacon chopped into
*   2.5cm/1 inch strips*
1 medium onion, sliced
4 stalks celery, diced
1 large cooking apple, chopped
1 orange, segmented and cubed
275ml/½ pint stock
575ml/1 pint cider

For the sauce:
cornflour
150ml/¼ pint cream

Pre-heat oven to 180°C/350°F/Gas Mark 4

---

1   Wipe the duck well with a damp cloth inside and out, and cut in half. Season the flour with a little salt and pepper and the finely chopped bay leaf. Roll the halves of duck in the flour.

---

2   Heat the oil over a low heat in a flame-proof casserole, add the birds and cook gently until they are browned all over. Remove the birds and set aside. Put the bacon and onion into the casserole and simmer until the onion becomes almost transparent.

---

3   Turn up the heat slightly and quickly stir-fry the celery, orange and apple until they are evenly mixed with the bacon and onion. Remove from the heat and return the birds to the casserole.

---

4   Add the stock and cider and place the dish in the oven for 1½ hours. If the casserole appears to be drying out during cooking, a little more cider can be added.

---

5   Remove the birds from the dish and set them aside to keep warm.

6 Put the casserole on top of the cooker over a low heat. Blend the cornflour with a little water and briskly stir this into the sauce and allow it to thicken. Carefully stir in the cream, remove from the heat and return the birds to the dish. This should be served as soon as possible after the addition of the cream.

To serve: Arrange the duck on individual dinner plates and spoon the sauce over them carefully.

Suggested accompaniment: Home-made potato croquettes and plain, buttered peas.

Duck Parcels

Serves 4   Cooking time: 40–50 minutes

450g/1lb cooked duck meat,
*   chopped*
40g/1½oz butter
100g/4oz bacon, chopped
100g/4oz mushrooms, sliced
25g/1oz flour
275ml/½ pint milk
salt and pepper
275g/10oz puff pastry

Pre-heat oven to 200°C/400°F/Gas Mark 6

---

1   Melt the butter in a pan over a low heat. Add the bacon and cook through.
     Stir in the mushrooms and toss until cooked lightly. Sprinkle on the flour.
     Stir well and allow to cook for 30 seconds. Gradually pour in the milk
     and stir continuously until thickened.

---

2   Add the duck, season with salt and pepper and heat through gently for 1–2
     minutes.

---

3   Roll out the pastry into 20cm×10cm/8in×4in rounds. Place a spoonful of
     the mixture in the centre of each round. Fold each in half to form a
     semi-circle and crimp the edge.

---

4   Glaze with a little milk or beaten egg. Cook in the oven for 25–30 minutes.

Suggested accompaniment: Baked potatoes and buttered broad beans.

Duck with Tarragon and Orange Mayonnaise

Serves 4   Resting time: 1 hour

700g/1½lb cooked duck meat
225g/8oz walnut halves
100g/4oz stuffed olives, sliced
pinch of cayenne
watercress to garnish

For the mayonnaise:
1 egg
5ml/1 teaspoon grainy mustard
30ml/2 tablespoons wine vinegar
2.5ml/½ teaspoon dried tarragon
rind ½ orange, sliced
approx. 175ml/⅓ pint olive or
   sunflower oil
salt and pepper

1   Break the egg into a blender, add the mustard, vinegar, tarragon, orange rind, salt and pepper. Liquidise for 20–30 seconds.

2   With blender running on low, gradually drip in the oil until the mayonnaise is the consistency you like.

3   Chop the duck into small pieces and spread on a large platter.

4   Stir the walnuts and the olives into the mayonnaise and carefully spoon this over the duck. Sprinkle with cayenne pepper and garnish with watercress sprigs. Chill for 1 hour.

Suggested accompaniment: Orange and rice salad (*see* Chapter 11).

Duck Croquettes

450g/1lb cooked duck
25g/1oz butter
1 onion, finely chopped
100g/4oz cooked ham
½ rind orange, grated
1 whole egg
1 beaten egg
flour
breadcrumbs
oil for frying
salt and pepper

1   Melt the butter over a low heat. Add the onion and cook gently until transparent.

2   Finely mince the duck and ham. Add the cooked onion and orange rind and mix well. Season with salt and pepper and bind the mixture with 1 egg.

3   Form the mixture into 12 croquettes and dip each portion into beaten egg. Roll lightly in the flour. Dip in beaten egg again and finally coat with breadcrumbs.

4   Heat some oil in a large frying pan and cook the croquettes until golden brown.

Suggested accompaniment: Baked potatoes and ratatouille.

CHAPTER 10

GEESE

It is illegal to sell wild geese. That is why you never see them in a game dealer's shop. And so, unless you have family or friends who are wildfowlers, you are unlikely to taste wild goose in Britain. You will be missing out, because a young goose can taste as good as mallard, some would say even better.

Many people who have never tasted a wild goose seem to think that they must taste fishy or of seaweed simply because they are associated with coastal areas. What they fail, however, to realise is that while the majority of geese roost at night on estuarine sandbanks, with only a small proportion resorting to inland waters such as Loch Leven, they seldom feed on the coast. Some may graze on fresh saltmarsh grasses, but the normal feeding grounds are inland pastures intended for farm livestock. They also glean the grain stubbles in late autumn and then move on to potato fields where waste tatties from the harvest remain to soften and rot in the winter frosts. In late winter and early spring they turn to fields of young winter wheat. So there is nothing fishy about the wild goose's diet.

As you would expect from birds that migrate south to us from the tundra grounds on the fringes of the Arctic, probably flying a total of twenty miles to and from their feeding grounds each day, geese are muscular birds. The meat is dark, closer-grained than that of game species and without a trace of fat, an important point to note when cooking.

Opinions on the length of time necessary to hang a goose are varied. Most feel, and I would agree with them, that unless the weather is unseasonably mild they require at least three weeks, and in cold weather you might double that figure. Geese are hung by the head, unplucked and undrawn, in a well-ventilated place. Remember to watch out for flies, as these may still be about even in November. As I have said in Chapter 8, a well-ventilated, fly-proof game larder can easily be constructed on the 'corner cupboard' principle (with the door and roof made of perforated gauze) in a garage or shed. This is a wise and very useful bit of DIY for a household that sees a lot of game, wildfowl and venison.

There are basically four species of geese that may be shot at the present time. These are the greylag and pinkfooted, the whitefronted (which may only be shot in England, being protected in Scotland), and the Canada, which was introduced as an ornamental bird but is now, as with so many species introduced to Britain, an agricultural pest.

A Canada has a black head and neck with white cheek patches that extend underneath and which may meet on the throat.

The other three species are all grey geese. The easiest way to identify them is by the colour of the bill. Pinkfoots have a black bill with a central pink band; greylags have an orange bill; the whitefront has a white forehead and the bill is fleshy-pink, becoming yellowish toward the base.

The greylag is the largest of the grey geese, though not as large as the Canada. It weighs from 2.5–4kg/5½–9½lb. The pinkfooted weighs from 2–4kg/4–8lb and the whitefront from 2–3kg/4–6lb.

As a rough and ready guide to age, I usually presume that a small, light bird will be a young one and that a heavier bird within the species' weight range will be older. Another method is to examine the tail feathers. In young birds these are notched in a 'V' shape, but only until about November, when they adopt their adult, rounded shape. When you have handled a few geese you will learn to recognise the less-defined body markings of a young bird (that become more distinct with age), and the rather paler shades of the bill, legs and feet.

Remember that while we think of a goose as a very large bird, capable of feeding a lot of people, it is really not that massive. The live weight of a small pinkfoot or whitefront is only 0.5kg/1lb more than that of a mallard drake, and the weight of edible meat will only be about 20 per cent of the original weight. So remember that your 3.5kg/7½lb greylag will only provide about 1kg/1½lb of actual meat, and don't invite a multitude to the feast!

Goose Terrine

Serves 6   Resting time: 8 hours   Cooking time: 2½ hours

Best kept in the fridge for 2 days before serving.

450g/1lb raw goose meat
30ml/2 tablespoons oil
1 large onion, finely chopped
2 garlic cloves, crushed
275ml/½ pint red wine
225g/8oz belly pork, cut into
    small pieces
50g/2oz bacon, chopped
5ml/1 teaspoon dried sage
5ml/1 teaspoon thyme
salt and pepper
bacon for lining the terrine

---

1   Cut the goose into small pieces. Season with salt and pepper. Pour the wine over and allow to steep for 8 hours.

Pre-heat oven to 170°C/325°F/Gas Mark 3

---

2   Heat the oil in a pan and add the onion. Cook gently until transparent. Add the garlic, belly pork and bacon. Continue cooking for 8–10 minutes over a low heat.

---

3   Strain the meat (reserving the liquor) and add to the pan with the sage and thyme. Brown lightly, stirring continuously.

---

4   Allow the mixture to cool slightly before putting in a liquidiser. Pour in the liquor and blend until smooth. Add more wine, if required.

---

5   Line the bottom and sides of a terrine with bacon and spoon in the mixture. Press down evenly. Place bacon rashers across the top. Cover with greaseproof or waxed paper and place the dish in a roasting tin half-filled with water. Cook in the oven for 2½ hours.

---

6   Leave to cool and keep in the fridge for 2 days before serving.

Suggested accompaniment: French bread and a green salad.

Roast Wild Goose

Serves 6   Cooking time: 2½–3 hours

1 wild goose
butter
1 large cooking apple
cloves
225g/½lb streaky bacon
stock
salt and pepper

Pre-heat oven to 180°C/350°F/Gas Mark 4

---

1   Wipe the bird inside and out with a clean, damp cloth. Place about 75g/3oz butter inside the goose.

---

2   Wash the cooking apple, stud it with a few cloves and place this in the cavity.

---

3   Rub the outside of the bird with plenty of butter and sprinkle with salt and pepper. Put the streaky bacon across the breast.

---

4   Place the goose inside a roastabag and turn it breast downwards. Pour 150ml/¼ pint stock into the bag and tie securely. Cook in oven for 2½–3 hours. The roastabag will help to ensure a more succulent bird. The goose should be checked every half hour, however, and if it appears to be drying out then a little more stock can be added through one of the holes in the bag.

---

5   At the end of 2½ hours slit the bag and turn the bird the right way up to brown for 20–30 minutes, basting every 10 minutes.

Suggested accompaniment: Crispy bacon rashers, game chips or roast potatoes, stuffing, gravy. Traditional turkey accompaniments would do well with goose; Brussels sprouts with chestnuts and watercress, plain buttered potatoes topped with parsley.

Roast Goose with Nut and Apple Stuffing

Serves 6–8   Cooking time: 3 hours 20 minutes

1 goose (4.5kg/10lb)
butter
1 onion, chopped
goose liver, finely chopped
100g/4oz breadcrumbs
150g/6oz cashew nuts
100g/4oz walnuts
800g/1lb cooking apples, peeled
*   and diced*
½ lemon rind, finely grated
5ml/1 teaspoon parsley
5ml/1 teaspoon oregano
flour
stock, made from giblets and a
*   few herbs*
150ml/¼ pint red wine
salt and pepper

Pre-heat oven to 180°C/350°F/Gas Mark 4

1   Melt a little butter in a pan and cook the onion until it is transparent. Add the chopped goose liver to the pan and cook through.

2   Grind the nuts to a fine texture (not powdery) and mix the onion and liver into them. Add the apples, rind, herbs and breadcrumbs, mixing well. Bind with the beaten egg. Season with salt and pepper.

3   Clean and dry the goose. Stuff the neck end of the bird with the nut mixture. Truss the goose and weigh it.

4   Cook for 20 minutes per lb (40 minutes per kg), basting occasionally. Remove the bird from the pan and keep warm. Strain off the excess fat from the roasting dish, add the flour, stock and wine to make a good gravy.

Suggested accompaniment: Buttered sprouts with almonds, fresh cranberries and roast potatoes.

Pot-Roasted Goose
with Pineapple and Peppers

Serves 6–8   Cooking time: approx. 2½–3 hours

1 goose (3–4kg/6–8lb)
75g/3oz butter
1 onion, finely chopped
2 green peppers
200g/7oz tin pineapple chunks in
*   syrup*
4 rashers bacon
10ml/2 teaspoons honey
150ml/¼ pint stock made from
*   the giblets*

Pre-heat oven to 150°C/300°F/Gas Mark 2

1   Melt 25g/1oz butter in a flame-proof casserole. Add the onion and cook gently for 3–4 minutes. Cut the peppers into strips, having removed all the seeds, and cook in the butter for 2–3 minutes.

2   Drain the pineapple and, reserving the syrup, stir the chunks into the onion and peppers. Mix well.

3   Place the bacon rashers across the breast, put the goose on top of the mixture and pour over half the reserved syrup and the stock. Cut the remaining butter into pieces and dot the bird with it.

4   Cover tightly and cook for 2–2½ hours in the oven until the bird is tender.

5   Mix the remaining syrup with the honey and brush the bird all over. Pour any left over syrup over the goose. Place the casserole in the oven, uncovered, and cook for a further 25–30 minutes.

To serve: Carve as usual. Spoon the fruit and vegetables over the top.

Suggested accompaniment: Braised Florence fennel, mushrooms and roast potatoes.

Goose in Cider

Serves 6   Cooking time: 3 hours

1 goose (approx. 3kg/7lb)
6 cloves
2 oranges
75g/3oz butter
100g/4oz bacon
575ml/1 pint dry cider
275ml/½ pint stock made from
*   giblets and 1 onion*
1 cooking apple

Pre-heat oven to 180°C/350°F/Gas Mark 4

1   Prod 1 orange all over with a fork. Stick in the cloves and place the orange inside the goose. Chop 25g/1oz butter into pieces and add to the body cavity. Secure with a skewer.

2   Melt the remaining butter in a pan and brush the bird all over. Tie the bacon rashers securely across the bird.

3   Place the bird breast-down in a roasting tin and pour over half the cider and the stock. Cook in the oven for 1½ hours. Baste occasionally.

4   Peel and chop the apple and peel and segment the orange. Add them to the roasting tin. Baste and continue cooking for 50 minutes.

5   Increase the heat to 200°C/400°F/Gas Mark 6. Turn the bird the right way up and pour the remaining cider over it. Cook for a further 20 minutes.

6   Remove the bacon from the bird and continue cooking for 15 minutes.

To serve: Carve the goose and pour the sauce over separately.

Suggested accompaniment: Game chips, braised celery and boiled beetroot.

Goose in Red Wine

Serves 6   Cooking time: 2½–3 hours

1 goose
100g/4oz butter
2 onions, chopped
100g/4oz bacon, chopped
450g/1lb mushrooms, sliced
275ml/½ pint red wine
salt and pepper

Pre-heat oven to 170°C/325°F/Gas Mark 3

---

1   Melt 50g/2oz butter in a large pan. Add the onion and cook for 3–4 minutes. Add the bacon and cook for a further 3 minutes. Carefully add the mushrooms and stir until they are coated with butter. Simmer for 1 minute.

---

2   Stuff the goose with the mushroom mixture.

---

3   Place the bird in a large casserole. Pour over the wine. Dot with the remaining butter and season with salt and pepper. Cover and cook in the oven for 2½–3 hours, basting occasionally. Remove the lid for the last 15 minutes of cooking to allow the bird to brown.

To serve: Carve the bird and serve with the mushroom stuffing. Make a thin gravy with the wine and a little stock.

Suggested accompaniment: Roast parsnips, braised celery and potato croquettes.

Pot-Roasted Goose with Mandarins

Serves 6   Cooking time: 2 hours 15 minutes

1 goose
75g/3oz butter
1 onion, chopped
425g/15oz can mandarin oranges
grated peel 1 orange
275ml/½ pint good stock
5ml/1 teaspoon cornflour
15ml/1 tablespoon brandy
pepper

Pre-heat oven to 170°C/325°F/Gas Mark 3

---

1   Melt 25g/1oz butter in a large, flame-proof casserole. Add the onion and cook for 2–3 minutes.

---

2   Drain the mandarins, reserving the syrup, and add them to the dish with the orange rind. Stir well.

---

3   Place the trussed goose on the fruit and dot with the remaining butter. Pour the syrup and stock over. Season with pepper. Cover and cook in the oven for 2 hours 15 minutes.

---

4   Remove the bird from the dish and keep warm.

---

5   Mix the cornflour to a smooth paste with a little water. Over a low heat add the cornflour to the sauce and stir until thickened. Pour in the brandy. Heat through.

To serve: Carve the goose and pour over the sauce

Suggested accompaniment: Roast potatoes, buttered peas with almonds.

Fricassee of Goose

Serves 4   Cooking time: 35 minutes

450g/1lb cooked goose
15g/½oz butter
1 bouquet garni
1 onion, chopped
575ml/1 pint good stock
grated peel ½ lemon
75ml/3fl oz cream
1 egg yolk
salt and pepper

1   Melt the butter in a pan. Add the onion and cook for 3–4 minutes.

2   Pour in the stock. Add the bouquet garni and lemon peel and season well with salt and pepper. Cover and simmer over a low heat for 25 minutes.

3   Cut the goose into cubes and add to the pan. Cook for 5 minutes or until warmed through.

4   Mix together the cream and the egg yolk.

5   Remove the pan from the heat and carefully stir in the cream and egg mixture. Very gently heat through, stirring to avoid curdling. Serve immediately.

Suggested accompaniment: Braised celery and mashed potato.

Hashed Goose

Serves 4   Cooking time: 55–60 minutes

450g/1lb cooked goose
50g/2oz butter
1 large onion, chopped
30ml/2 tablespoons port
575ml/1 pint stock
15ml/1 tablespoon rowan jelly
10ml/2 teaspoons cornflour
salt and pepper

Pre-heat oven to 150°C/300°F/Gas Mark 2

1   Melt the butter in a pan. Add the onion and cook gently for 3–4 minutes.

2   Cut the goose into small cubes and place them in a casserole. Add the onion, port, stock and jelly. Season with salt and pepper. Cover and cook in the oven for 40 minutes.

3   Mix the cornflour to a smooth paste with a little water and add it to the casserole. Mix well, cover and continue cooking for a further 15 minutes.

Suggested accompaniment: Buttered noodles or rice.

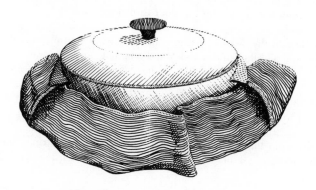

Grander Gander

A classic recipe for dealing with an old goose.

Serves 4   Cooking time: 45 minutes

1 old goose
2 onions
2 potatoes
3 carrots
1 small turnip
225g/8oz bacon
50g/2oz butter
30ml/2 tablespoons flour
850ml/1½ pints stock
70ml/2½fl oz red wine
1 tablespoon parsley
1 bouquet garni
salt and pepper
2 newspapers (tabloids are too
   small)

1   Peel and finely chop the onions, potatoes, carrots and turnip. Reserve the peelings. Cut the rind from the bacon. Finely chop the bacon. Reserve the rind.

2   Melt the butter in a pan and add the vegetables and bacon. Simmer gently for 15 minutes. Sprinkle on the flour to make a roux.

3   Gradually add the stock, stirring continuously. Bring to the boil. Reduce the heat and add the wine, parsley and bouquet garni. Season with salt and pepper. Allow to simmer for 30 minutes. Pour this into a thermos flask.

4   Spread out the newspapers. Place the gander in the middle of the papers. Surround with the peelings and bacon rind.

5   Carefully wrap the goose in the paper and secure with string. Dig a large hole in the garden, or preferably someone else's garden, and bury the package.

6   Pour yourself a cup of soup from the thermos while you forget where you buried it!

CHAPTER 11

THE MIXED BAG

This final chapter includes a variety of recipes, some of them using up an assortment of meat in the form of soup or game pies. There are accompaniments which, in the form of stuffings, vegetables and sauces, whether traditional or new, are essential contributions towards any meal, whether for every day or for that special occasion.

Most towns now host a supermarket stocked full with good, fresh vegetables and some varieties that, in days gone by, were only available in the more exclusive shops. While there will always be room for the frozen pea, it is good to know that the choice is there if you wish it. And your local wholefood shop may be like mine, an Aladdin's cave filled with such a selection of herbs and spices that I more often than not come out having spent twice what I intended.

These outlets often provide leaflets and instructions on what to do with the more unusual vegetable, fruit or spice and it is partly due to this that we have become more cosmopolitan in our tastes and less reluctant to experiment. That must be good for us all – especially for the cookery writer!

Game Stock

This will really depend on what is available to you at the time. As stock is the basic ingredient for so many recipes, however, the flavour is all important and it is worth collecting an assortment of game, storing it in the freezer until you have sufficient. If you only require a small amount the quantities below can be reduced.

Makes approx. 3 litres/5 pints   Cooking time: 3 hours

1 old pheasant
1 pigeon or other game bird
1 rabbit
1 piece venison
1 small ham shank
2 onions, halved
2 carrots, halved
3 sticks celery, halved
1 bay leaf
1 bouquet garni
1 small bunch parsley
salt and pepper
water (approx. 3 litres/5 pints)

---

1   Cut the birds in half. Joint the rabbit and place it with the birds, venison and ham shank in a large pot.

---

2   Put the vegetables and herbs in the pot and season well with salt and pepper.

---

3   Add sufficient water to cover the meat and vegetables. Cover with a lid and bring to the boil. Remove any scum that forms and simmer the stock for 3 hours.

---

4   Allow to cool before straining. Remove any meat from the bones, liquidise and blend back into the stock. (Alternatively the meat can be reserved for currying.)

Quick Spicy Game Soup

Serves 6–8   Cooking time: 50 minutes

450g/1lb minced game (assorted)
100g/4oz butter
2 large onions, chopped
100g/4oz belly pork, chopped
1kg/2lb 3oz tinned tomatoes
1 red pepper, deseeded and
    chopped
1 green pepper, deseeded and
    chopped
1kg/2lb 3oz tinned red kidney
    beans, drained
450g/1lb tinned chick peas,
    drained
850ml/1½ pints stock
7.5ml/1½ teaspoons chilli powder
2.5ml/½ teaspoon salt

1   Melt the butter in a large pan. Add the onion and the belly pork and cook until slightly coloured. Add the game and continue cooking until well-browned.

2   Add the tomatoes, peppers, beans, and chick peas. Pour in the stock and stir well. Season with chilli powder and salt. Cover and simmer for 35 minutes. Allow to cool.

3   Pour the soup into a liquidiser and blend thoroughly.

4   Return to the pan and, stirring continuously, allow to heat through.

Suggested accompaniment: Garlic bread.

Crawford's Game Soup

When my husband 'creates a masterpiece' in the kitchen, it usually is just that. He takes on the role of Mr Bridges admirably and with an enthusiasm that I, as regular 'food processor', fail to aspire to. Unfortunately this role-change finds me acting as Ruby for a considerable time afterwards in the 'bomb site', but it is surely worth the effort, especially where the following recipe is concerned!

Serves 12   Cooking time: 3 hours

1 hare
2 game birds
100g/4oz butter
2 onions, chopped
1 leek, chopped
4 sticks celery, chopped
1 turnip, chopped
3 carrots, chopped
2 bay leaves
1 bouquet garni
salt and pepper
50g/2oz flour
150ml/¼ pint port
275ml/½ pint red wine
30ml/2 tablespoons tomato purée
3 litres/5 pints water (approx.
   enough to cover ingredients)

1   Joint the hare and halve the birds. Melt 50g/2 oz butter in a large pan over a moderate heat. Add the hare and birds and brown them. Add the onions, leek and celery to the pan. Cook until the onion is transparent. Add the turnip, carrot, bay leaves and bouquet garni. Season well with salt and pepper.

2   Pour in just sufficient water to cover the contents in the pan (roughly 3 litres/5 pints). Bring to the boil. Remove any scum that forms with a slotted spoon. Reduce heat to simmer, cover and cook for 2½ hours or until the meat is tender.

3   Strain the stock through a fine sieve and leave to cool.

4   Remove the bay leaf and bouquet garni from the meat and vegetables. Take the meat off the bones. Place the meat and vegetables in a liquidiser with a little of the stock and blend to a thick purée.

5   Melt the remaining butter over a moderate heat in a large pan. Blend in the flour stirring continuously, and allow to brown slightly. Remove from the heat and gradually add the port, wine, tomato purée and 575 litres/1 pint of the stock.

6   Return the pan to the heat and simmer. Blend in the meat and vegetable purée and the remaining stock. Stir continuously until the soup is thickened and hot. Adjust seasoning if required. Serve.

To serve: Serve with fresh, crusty French bread.

Mixed Game Crustades

Serves 4 Cooking time: 10–15 minutes

100g/4oz mixed cooked game,
  chopped
15g/½oz butter
50g/2oz bacon, finely chopped
2 shallots, finely chopped
275ml/½ pint white sauce
French bread stick
50g/2oz grated cheese

Pre-heat oven to 200°C/400°F/Gas Mark 6

1 Melt the butter in a small pan. Add the bacon and shallots and cook until lightly golden. Mix this with the white sauce. Add the cooked game.

2 Cut 8x3cm/1½in slices from the bread stick. Push out the white so that you are left with the circular crusts.

3 Place the crusts on a baking sheet and fill the middle with the game and white sauce mixture. Sprinkle with grated cheese and cook in the oven for 10 minutes or until golden brown.

To serve: Garnish with chopped parsley and serve as a starter. The filling can also be used for vol-au-vent cases.

Game Cocktail

Serves 6   Preparation time: 10 minutes

100g/4oz cooked game, chopped
50g/2oz cooked ham, chopped
275ml/½ pint mayonnaise
5ml/1 teaspoon Worcester sauce
2 gherkins, chopped
5ml/1 teaspoon chives, chopped
1 apple, peeled and chopped
½ avocado, peeled and chopped
1 head chicory, finely shredded
cayenne pepper
lemon wedges
salt and pepper

1   Mix together the mayonnaise and Worcester sauce, season with salt and pepper. Add the gherkins, chives, apple, avocado, ham and game. Mix well.

2   Divide the chicory into 6 serving dishes to form a shallow bed. Spoon the mixture on to the chicory.

3   Sprinkle well with cayenne pepper and garnish each dish with a lemon wedge.

To serve: Serve the game cocktail as a starter.

Easy Game Pie

Serves 6–8   Cooking time: 1½ hours

1kg/2lb assorted game, cut into
  cubes, (e.g. venison, grouse,
  rabbit, hare, pheasant)
seasoned flour
225g/8oz bacon, cut into small
  strips
1 large onion
stock made from the bones and
  giblets
red wine
salt and pepper
75g/3oz butter
350g/12oz shortcrust pastry

Pre-heat oven to 180°C/350°F/Gas Mark 4

1   Melt the butter in a heavy-based pan or casserole.

2   Coat the game pieces in seasoned flour and brown gently with the bacon. Slice the onion, add it to the pan and cook for a couple of minutes.

3   Put this mixture into a casserole, adding enough stock and red wine to cover. Season with salt and pepper. Place the casserole in the oven and cook for 1–1½ hours, adding more liquid if required.

4   Line a pie dish with pastry. Put the cooked mixed game into the pie dish with a little stock and cover with a pastry lid. Finish cooking.

To serve: This dish is delicious hot but I prefer it cold and cut into wedges. It makes a filling addition to the picnic box and is ideal for shooting lunches.

Orange Gravy

Serves 4–6   Cooking time: 5–10 minutes

50ml/¼ pint fresh orange juice
grated rind one orange
squeeze lemon juice
30ml/2 tablespoons port
30ml/2 tablespoons redcurrant
  jelly
a little double cream
caster sugar to taste

1 Pour off the excess fat from the roasting tin. Add the orange juice, lemon juice and grated rind and simmer for several minutes.

2 Pour in the port and stir in the redcurrant jelly. Add sugar to taste, if necessary, allowing this to dissolve.

3 Reduce the heat and quickly add a little double cream. Stirring continuously, reheat slowly, not allowing it to boil. Serve immediately.

To serve: This can be served with any game bird.

Demi-Glacé Sauce for Game

150ml/¼ pint jellied game stock
150ml/½ pint espagnole sauce
  (see page 200)
70ml/2½fl oz sherry or Madeira

1 Strain the espagnole sauce through a sieve. Pour into a pan with the stock. Bring to the boil and, stirring continuously, cook until the sauce is thick and shiny.

2 Stir in the sherry or Madeira and serve.

To serve: Serve as a sauce with any game.

Suggested accompaniment: Herby pheasant croquettes etc.

Asparagus and Mushroom Sauce

Serves 6   Cooking time: 20–30 minutes

350–450g/¾–1lb chopped
  mushrooms
425ml/¾ pint water
175ml/6fl oz cup of milk
225g/8oz thinly, diagonally cut
  asparagus
60ml/4 tablespoons butter
100g/4oz chopped onion
1 clove garlic, crushed
60ml/4 tablespoons flour
2.5ml/½ teaspoon tarragon
salt and pepper to taste

For the topping:
grated Parmesan (optional)

---

1   Salt the mushrooms lightly and steam them for 10 minutes in the water. Drain them and press out all excess liquid. Measure the liquid and add enough milk to make up to 850ml/1½ pints.

---

2   Cook the asparagus in a steamer for 10 minutes or so until it is the preferred consistency.

---

3   Melt the butter, add the onions and garlic. When onions become soft, whisk in the flour. Cook over low heat for 5 minutes, whisking all the time. Add the liquid from the mushrooms.

---

4   Continue to cook over a low heat, stirring frequently for about 8–10 minutes, until the sauce thickens. Add the mushrooms, asparagus and tarragon. Season to taste.

Madeira Sauce

Serves 4   Cooking time: 20 minutes

50g/2oz butter
50g/2oz bacon, finely chopped
1 onion, finely chopped
15ml/1 tablespoon flour
4 ripe tomatoes, peeled and
*   chopped*
2.5ml/½ teaspoon fresh basil
100g/4oz mushrooms, chopped
275ml/½ pint stock
70ml/2½fl oz Madeira (or sherry)
sugar (optional)
salt and pepper

1   Melt the butter in a saucepan. Add the bacon and onion and cook until golden brown. Stir in the flour to make a roux. Cook for 1 minute.

2   Add the tomatoes, herbs and mushrooms. Gradually combine the stock. Cover and simmer for 10 minutes.

3   Pour in the Madeira. Season to taste, adding a little sugar if necessary. Cover and continue to simmer for 5–10 minutes.

Suggested accompaniment: Roast snipe or any game bird.

Espagnole Sauce for Game

Cooking time: 1½ hours

50g/2oz butter
1 carrot, finely chopped
1 onion, finely chopped
2 celery sticks, finely chopped
75g/3oz bacon, finely chopped
50g/2oz flour
575ml/1 pint game stock
1 bouquet garni
45ml/3 tablespoons tomato purée
5ml/1 teaspoon sugar
salt and pepper

1   Melt the butter in a pan over a low heat. Add the chopped vegetables and bacon and cook gently for 10–15 minutes.

2   Blend in the flour to make a roux. Gradually stir in 425ml/¾ pint of stock. Season with salt and pepper and add the bouquet garni. Cover and simmer on lowest possible heat for 45 minutes.

3   Add the remaining stock, purée and sugar. Cover and continue to simmer for 30 minutes.

To serve: Serve as a sauce with any game.

Garlic Mayonnaise Sauce

(This recipe was given to me by Kathy Berman)

Serves 6

150ml/¼ pint fresh, squeezed
  lemon juice
2.5ml/½ teaspoon salt
5ml/1 teaspoon tamari
3 medium cloves garlic, crushed
2 whole eggs
2 egg yolks
850ml/1½ pints oil (use all or
  part olive oil)

---

1   Blend all the ingredients except the oil thoroughly, at high speed in a blender. Turn the blender speed down to medium.

---

2   Gradually drip in the oil. Keep the blender running at medium until all the oil is incorporated. The mixture should be thick. Switch off immediately.

Suggested accompaniment: As above.

Bread Sauce

Makes approx. 425ml/¾ pint   Preparation time: 30 minutes

1 onion
6 cloves
6 peppercorns
575ml/1 pint milk
50g/2oz butter
salt
75g/3oz breadcrumbs

1   Make a cut just halfway through the onion from the side, rather than from top to tail (which prevents the onion from breaking up).

2   Stud the onion with the cloves and place it in a pan with the peppercorns, milk and 25g/1oz of butter.

3   Heat the milk slowly over a *low heat* and allow to simmer for 20 minutes. Cover with a lid and allow the milk to become quite cool. Remove the clove-studded onion.

4   Reheat the milk over a low heat. Stir in the breadcrumbs and mix well. Beat in the remaining butter and season with salt. (If you have time, allow the sauce to rest for 1–2 hours after cooking, then return the onion to the pan and reheat and remove the onion just prior to serving.)

To serve: Serve with any game bird, and with a warning to avoid the peppercorns!

Cumberland Sauce

Makes 1 pint   Resting time: 12 hours   Cooking time: 10 minutes

2 oranges
2 lemons
225g/8oz rowan jelly

225g/8oz redcurrant jelly
200ml/7fl oz port

1   Pare the peel carefully from 1 orange and 1 lemon and cut it into very fine strips. Boil in a little water for 2 minutes. Strain.

2   Squeeze the juice from the fruits and put in a pan with the rowan and redcurrant jelly. Simmer gently for 2–3 minutes. Pour in the port and bring to the boil. Remove from the heat.

3   Add the strips of peel. Stir well and chill for 12 hours before serving.

Suggested accompaniment: Any cold game.

Walnut, Apple and Raisin Sauce

Serves 4   Cooking time: 5–10 minutes

450g/1lb cooking apples, peeled,
    cored and diced
150ml/¼ pint medium cider
50g/2oz chopped walnuts
50g/2oz raisins

1   Place the apples in a pan with the cider and simmer until it is a thick pulp.

2   Add the walnuts and raisins and more cider if necessary. Simmer for 5–10 minutes. A little sugar may be added if it is too tart.

To serve: This sauce can be served hot or cold and is excellent not only with game but as an alternative to the usual apple sauce with pork and ham.

Piazzaiola Sauce

Serves 6   Cooking time: 40 minutes

30ml/2 tablespoons oil
2 onions, finely chopped
2 garlic cloves, crushed
1 red pepper, finely chopped
1 green pepper, finely chopped
5ml/1 teaspoon oregano
10ml/2 teaspoons basil
425g/15oz tin tomatoes, chopped
100g/4oz mushrooms, sliced
dash of tabasco
4 black olives, quartered
salt and pepper

1   Heat the oil in a pan. Add the onion and cook gently for 5 minutes. Add the garlic, peppers and herbs. Cook for a further 5 minutes.

2   Pour in the tomatoes, mushrooms and tabasco. Allow to simmer for 30 minutes.

3   Season with salt and pepper and stir in the olives. Heat through and serve.

Suggested accompaniment: Any grilled or roasted meat or game.

Pepper Sauce

Serves 6   Resting time: 2 hours   Cooking time: 30–40 minutes

50g/2oz butter
1 stick celery, finely chopped
1 onion, finely chopped
1 carrot, finely chopped
25g/1oz flour
575ml/1 pint good game or beef
   stock
150ml/½ pint red wine
5 peppercorns, crushed
15ml/1 tablespoon tomato purée
15ml/1 tablespoon parsley,
   chopped
70ml/2½fl oz single cream

---

1   Heat the butter over a low heat. Add the celery, onion and carrot. Cook gently for 10 minutes.

---

2   Add the flour and brown slightly before blending in the stock and red wine.

---

3   Stir in peppercorns and purée. Allow to simmer gently for 25 minutes. Let the sauce rest for 2 hours to allow the flavours to develop.

---

4   Reheat gently over a low heat and adjust seasoning if required. Just before serving add the cream and the chopped parsley. Heat through, stirring continuously. Do not boil.

Suggested accompaniment: Venison, but pepper sauce is good with most game.

Velouté Sauce

Serves 4–6   Cooking time: 55 minutes

40g/1½oz butter
40g/1½oz flour
850ml/1½ pints stock, warm
salt and pepper
45ml/3 tablespoons double cream

---

1   Melt the butter in a pan over a low heat. Add the flour and blend to make a roux.

---

2   Gradually add the warm stock and, stirring continuously, bring to the boil. Season with salt and pepper. Reduce heat and allow to simmer until reduced by half (approximately 50 minutes).

---

3   Remove the pan from the heat and strain the sauce through a muslin or fine sieve.

---

4   Beat in the cream.

To serve: Serve as a sauce with any game.

French Dressing

Resting time: 1 hour

150ml/¼ pint olive or sunflower
*   oil*
50ml/2 fl oz wine vinegar
15ml/1 tablespoon vinegar
5ml/1 teaspoon grainy French
*   mustard*
2.5ml/½ teaspoon salt
a few twists black pepper
5–10ml/1–2 teaspoons caster
*   sugar*

---

1   Put all the ingredients into a screw top jar. Shake vigorously until well
     blended.

---

2   Chill well for 1 hour before use.

To serve: The dressing will keep well in the fridge for a week or two. Serve
with a large salad.

Variations on French Dressing

Tarragon Dressing

Resting time: 1 hour

200ml/⅓ pint French dressing
40ml/2 dessertspoons chopped
*   tarragon*

---

1   Put the chopped tarragon into a jar with French dressing. Shake vigorously until well blended.

---

2   Chill well for 1 hour before use.

Suggested accompaniment: Grilled pheasant and salad, or with any game.

Garlic Dressing

Resting time: 1 hour

200ml/⅓ pint French dressing
1–2 cloves garlic, crushed

---

1   Put the garlic into a jar with French dressing. Shake vigorously until well blended.

---

2   Chill well for 1 hour before use.

Suggested accompaniment: As above.

Herb Dressings

Resting time: 1 hour

200ml/⅓ pint French dressing
40ml/2 dessertspoons fresh chives
   (or basil, or mint, or
   coriander, or 1 green chilli),
   chopped

---

1   Add one of the above ingredients to French dressing to make an assortment
    of dressings. Shake vigorously until well blended.

---

2   Chill well for 1 hour before use.

Suggested accompaniment: As above.

Tarragon and Orange Mayonnaise

Serves 6

1 egg
5ml/1 teaspoon grainy mustard
30ml/2 tablespoons wine vinegar
rind ½ orange, sliced
2.5ml/½ teaspoon dried tarragon
salt and pepper
approx. 200ml/⅓ pint olive or
   sunflower oil

---

1   Break the egg into a blender. Add the mustard, vinegar, tarragon, orange
    rind, salt and pepper. Liquidise for 20–30 seconds.

---

2   With blender running on low, gradually drip in the oil until the mayonnaise
    is the consistency you like.

Suggested accompaniment: Duck with walnuts and olives.

Herby Mayonnaise

Serves 6

1 whole egg
15ml/1 tablespoon good wine
    vinegar (I like to make my own
    to get a good mixture of spices)
5ml/1 teaspoon grainy mustard
a few twists of pepper

salt
squeeze lemon juice
5ml/1 teaspoon tarragon
2.5ml/½ teaspoon chopped
    parsley
olive oil

1   Put all but the olive oil into the liquidiser and blend quickly for 2–3 seconds.

2   Turn the liquidiser to a high speed and gradually drip in the oil through the top – the amount of this will depend upon the preferred consistency.

To serve: Serve with a green salad and any game dish.

Waldorf Salad

Serves 4   Resting time: 1 hour

3 sticks celery, chopped
2 red-skinned apples, cored and
    chopped
50g/2oz walnut halves
50g/2oz shelled peanuts

45ml/3 tablespoons mayonnaise
30ml/1 tablespoon French
    dressing
salt and pepper
pinch of cayenne

1   Place the celery, apple and nuts in a bowl.

2   Mix together the mayonnaise and French dressing. Season with a little salt and a twist of pepper. Pour over the salad and mix well.

3   Sprinkle the salad with a pinch of cayenne pepper. Chill for 1 hour.

Suggested accompaniment: All cold roast game or pies.

Chicory and Orange Salad

Serves 6   Resting time: 1 hour

1 large orange
30ml/2 tablespoons natural
*   yoghurt*
45ml/3 tablespoons mayonnaise
2.5ml/¹/₂ teaspoon Dijon mustard
1 head chicory
50g/2oz walnuts, chopped
1 bunch watercress
pepper

1   Grate the orange rind into a small bowl. Add the yoghurt, mayonnaise and mustard, mixing well. Chill for 1 hour.

2   Peel the orange and remove all the pith. Cut the segments into small pieces.

3   Finely shred the chicory into a large bowl. Add the oranges and walnuts. Carefully mix in the dressing. Season with a little pepper.

4   Chop the watercress and sprinkle on to the salad.

Suggested accompaniment: Good with any cold game.

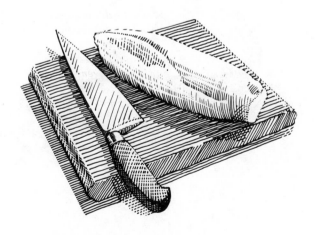

Orange and Rice Salad

Serves 4–6   Resting time: 1 hour   Cooking time: 15 minutes

8oz/225g long grain rice
2 oranges, peeled and segmented
¼ cucumber
45ml/3 tablespoons French
   dressing
salt and pepper

1   Boil the rice and allow to cool.

2   Chop the oranges finely, removing all the pith and stones. Slice the cucumber into small cubes.

3   Mix together the rice, orange and cucumber. Season well with salt and pepper and stir in the French dressing.

4   Mix well and chill for 1 hour before serving.

Suggested accompaniment: Any cold game.

Game Chips

Serves 4–6   Cooking time: 15 minutes

700g/1½lb potatoes
oil for frying

Pre-heat oven to 200°C/400°F/Gas Mark 6

1   Peel the potatoes and slice them very thinly. Place the slices in a colander and run the cold tap briskly over them for 2–3 minutes to help the pieces separate and remove the excess starch. Dry on a kitchen towel.

2   Heat some oil in a chip pan and, a few at a time, add the potato slices. Fry until golden brown and crisp.

3   Place potatoes on a piece of kitchen roll and keep warm in the oven for 15 minutes or until they are ready.

Suggested accompaniment: Grilled pheasant, roast grouse, stuffed woodcock.

Cheater's Game Chips

Serves 4   Cooking time: 3–5 minutes

2 packets salted crisps

Pre-heat oven to 200°C/400°F/Gas Mark 6

1   Spread the crisps on a baking sheet and place in the oven to warm through for a few minutes.

2   Remove from the oven and serve.

Game Straws

Serves 4–6   Cooking time: 15 minutes

700g/1½lb potatoes
oil for frying

Pre-heat oven to 200°C/400°F/Gas Mark 6

---

1   Peel the potatoes and cut into thin, mini chips. Place in a colander and run the cold tap briskly over them for 2–3 minutes to help the pieces separate and remove the excess starch. Dry on a kitchen towel.

---

2   Heat some oil in a chip pan and, a few at a time, add the potato chips. Fry until golden brown and crisp.

---

3   Place potatoes on a piece of kitchen roll and keep warm in the oven for 15 minutes.

Suggested accompaniment: Herby pheasant croquettes and sauerkraut, hareburgers.

Cheater's Game Straws

Serves 4   Cooking time: 3–5 minutes

2 packets salted potato chiplets

Pre-heat oven to 200°C/400°F/Gas Mark 6

---

1   Spread the chiplets on a baking sheet and place in the oven to warm though for a few minutes.

---

2   Remove from the oven and serve.

Forcemeat

My mother-in-law, Catherine Little, gave me this and the following recipe which she used with turkey. They are equally good with game and wildfowl.

50g/2oz white breadcrumbs
50g/2oz brown breadcrumbs
50g/2oz shredded suet
30ml/2 tablespoons parsley,
   chopped

2.5ml/½ teaspoon mixed herbs
2.5ml/½ teaspoon grated nutmeg
2 lemon rinds, grated finely
salt and pepper
1 large or 2 small eggs

1   Mix all the dry ingredients together in a bowl.

2   Beat the eggs and stir into the forcemeat to bind.

To serve: Fills half a turkey or any whole, medium-sized game bird.

Chestnut Stuffing

1kg/2lb 3oz chestnuts
milk and water for boiling
275ml/½ pint stock
salt and pepper

pinch of cinnamon/nutmeg
5ml/1 teaspoon caster sugar
50g/2oz butter

1   Make a small slit in the chestnut skins with a sharp knife. Place them in a pan. Add a mixture of 1 part milk to 3 parts water, sufficient to cover. Boil for 20 minutes.

2   Drain the nuts into a colander and run the cold tap over them briskly until they are cool. Remove the skins.

3   Mash the chestnuts well and put them in a pan with the stock. Simmer until tender.

4   Season with salt, pepper, cinnamon, nutmeg and sugar. Stir in the butter to bind well.

To serve: Fills half a turkey, or any medium-sized game bird.

Nut and Apple Stuffing

25g/1oz butter
1 onion, chopped
150g/6oz cashew nuts
250g/8oz apples, peeled and
*   chopped*
1/2 lemon rind, finely grated
5ml/1 teaspoon parsley
5ml/1 teaspoon oregano
100g/4oz breadcrumbs
1 egg, beaten
salt and pepper

1   Melt the butter in a pan. Add the onion and cook gently until transparent.

2   Grind the nuts to a fine texture (not powdery) and mix with the onion and butter.

3   Add the apples, rind, herbs and breadcrumbs. Season with salt and pepper and bind with the beaten egg.

To serve: Good with all game birds and wildfowl. This is enough stuffing for one medium-sized bird.

Nut Stuffing

(This recipe was given to me by Alison Turnbull)

butter
1 large onion, finely chopped
250g/9oz Brazil nuts
175g/6oz almonds
250g/9oz toasted cashews
7.5ml/1½ teaspoons sage

5ml/1 teaspoon oregano
22.5ml/1½ tablespoons parsley
75g/3oz breadcrumbs
rind and juice 1 orange
1 egg, beaten
salt and pepper

1   Soften the onion in a little butter over a low heat.

2   Remove the onion from the pan and put into a large mixing bowl.

3   Grind up the nuts so that they are fine but not powdery and add them to the onions, along with the herbs, breadcrumbs, rind and juice. Bind the mixture with an egg and season with salt and pepper.

To serve: Serve as a stuffing for any medium-sized game bird or wildfowl.

Sage, Onion and Orange Stuffing

100g/4oz onions, finely chopped
15ml/1 tablespoon sage, chopped
1 orange rind, finely chopped
50g/2oz fresh breadcrumbs
15ml/1 tablespoon orange
  marmalade
25g/1oz melted butter to bind
salt and pepper

1   Mix together all the ingredients.

2   Bind with the butter if necessary.

To serve: As above.

Redcurrant Jelly

Cooking time: 2 hours 20 minutes

2.7kg/6lb redcurrants
1.7 litres/3 pints water
preserving sugar

1   Place the redcurrants in a pan with 1.1 litres/2 pints water. Simmer for 30 minutes or until tender. Strain the fruit through a muslin or jelly-bag and allow to drip into a bowl for 10–15 minutes. Do not squeeze the bag as this makes the syrup cloudy.

2   Return the redcurrants to the pan with 0.5 litres/1 pint water. Simmer for a further 25 minutes. Strain this second extract into the jelly-bag and allow it to drip for at least 1 hour.

3   Measure the liquid and allow 450g/1lb sugar for each pint of juice.

4   Place the juice and sugar in a jam pan. Bring to the boil and boil rapidly for approximately 10 minutes until setting point is reached. Test for this by putting 5ml/1 teaspoonful of jelly on to a cold saucer. Once cool, push the jelly with your finger and if the skin wrinkles the jelly is ready.

5   Remove any scum that forms with a slotted spoon. Pour the jelly into warmed, clean jars. Cover immediately with waxed discs and cellophane covers.

Suggested accompaniment: Casserole of grouse, roast venison etc.

Rowan Jelly

Cooking time: 2 hours 40–50 minutes

2.7kg/6lb rowan berries
1.7litres/3 pints water
sugar

Proceed as for redcurrant jelly but allow the first stage of simmering approximately 50–60 minutes.

Suggested accompaniment: Roast grouse à la Rob Roy, stuffed woodcock etc.

Pickled Peaches

Cooking time: 15 minutes

1.8kg/4lb peaches, peeled, stoned
*   and quartered*
425ml/3/4 pint spiced vinegar
225g/8oz sugar

1   Heat the vinegar to simmering point. Add the sugar and stir until dissolved. Add the peaches and simmer gently for 15 minutes.

2   Remove the peaches and pack into warm, clean jars.

3   Boil the syrup until it has reduced and thickened slightly (approximately 3 minutes). Remove any scum with kitchen towel. Pour the syrup over the fruit. Seal immediately.

Suggested accompaniments: Roast grouse à la Rob Roy, hare curry.

Spiced Vinegar

Resting time: 3 months

*575ml/1 pint malt vinegar (best
    for pickling)*
8 black peppercorns
small piece root ginger
6 cloves
1 cinnamon stick
1 bay leaf
1.5ml/¼ teaspoon salt

1   Place all the spices with the vinegar in a bottle. Shake well.

2   Allow to stand for at least 3 months, shaking occasionally.

Suggested accompaniment: Hare curry, venison burgers.

Spiced Vinegar Quick Method

This recipe is quick but not as good as the previous one. If you are suddenly the beneficiary of goodies to be pickled, however, there is no point in being pernickety!

Resting time: 4 hours   Cooking time: 10 minutes

*Ingredients as for the above
    recipe.*

1   Put all the ingredients into a bowl in a pan of water.

2   Bring the pan to the boil. Cover the bowl. Remove the pan from the heat and allow the vinegar to stand in the water for 4 hours.

3   Remove the spices from the vinegar and bottle ready for use.

INDEX